Dear Reader,

Sometimes I don't realize what a small world we live in. I currently live in a tiny town, but recently I met someone who lived in the place where I spent much of my childhood—in a town that's almost a thousand miles away. Small world.

As small as the world is, sometimes life circumstances carry us away from friends we care about and we never see them again. This was what childhood sweethearts Cristóbal and Viviani thought would happen when one of their families relocated, taking them far away from the other. As hard as it was, they both moved on with their lives. But fate and that whole small-world thing intervened almost twenty years later, when Cris and Vivi found themselves back in the same town. Both of them have had their share of heartaches in the intervening years and have no intention of rekindling a romance with anyone...but...

With the story set in the beautiful backdrops of Santiago and Valparaiso, Chile, join this couple as they navigate the waters of the past and get carried into the present. Not without some very real struggles, though.

Love,

Tina Beckett

SECOND CHANCE IN SANTIAGO

TINA BECKETT

Harlequin

MEDICAL ROMANCE

Harlequin®
MEDICAL
ROMANCE

Recycling programs
for this product may
not exist in your area.

ISBN-13: 978-1-335-94311-8

Second Chance in Santiago

Harlequin Enterprises ULC
22 Adelaide St. West, 41st Floor
Toronto, Ontario M5H 4E3, Canada
www.Harlequin.com

Printed in U.S.A.

Three-time Golden Heart® Award finalist **Tina Beckett** learned to pack her suitcases almost before she learned to read. Born to a military family, she has lived in the United States, Puerto Rico, Portugal and Brazil. In addition to traveling, Tina loves to cuddle with her pug, Alex; spend time with her family; and hit the trails on her horse. Learn more about Tina from her website or friend her on Facebook.

Visit the Author Profile page
at Harlequin.com for more titles.

To my family. I love you!

**Praise for
Tina Beckett**

"Tina Beckett definitely followed through on the
premise and managed to infuse just the right amount
of angst and passion to keep me glued to the pages of
Miracle Baby for the Midwife from beginning to end."
—*Harlequin Junkie*

PROLOGUE

CRISTÓBAL DIAZ ARRIVED just in time to see a vehicle packed with stuff parked at the curb. But that wasn't what caught his attention: it was the person in the back seat—his high school sweetheart. They'd agreed to let last night at the park be their final goodbye, but he hadn't been able to stand the thought that it might be the final time he saw her. And today he'd been compelled by his emotions to come here.

But was this any better?

Vivi's dad frowned at him, letting him know that his presence wasn't exactly welcome, but that was nothing new. He'd never thought Cris was good enough for his only daughter. The problem was that Cris agreed with the man.

She'd been crying, as evidenced by her red eyes and the way she swiped her palm over the moisture on her cheek. And his chest contracted at the thought he might be the cause of that pain. It probably would have been better if he'd never given her that ring with the little red crystals last Christmas, the only thing he could afford on his salary at the local grocery store. She'd tried to give it back to him last night, but he'd placed it back in her palm, curling her fingers over the thin gold band.

He would never get over her. Ever. They would both go on with their lives, because there was no choice, and time didn't stop. Not for him. Not for Vivi. And not for whatever the future might have held for them if her father's change in his diplomatic posting hadn't happened. Vivi said it had been mandatory, and that may have been true, but he was pretty sure her dad wasn't unhappy about being relocated to Santiago. Before they moved there, though, they were going back to the United States for vacation. Vivi's mom was American, but Arturo had been a Chilean exchange student in Kansas, where the couple had met. Vivi was born soon after they were married. He was now a US citizen and had worked his way up the ranks in government work.

And Mrs. Araya, although she'd never disliked him, wouldn't quite meet his eyes right now, so Cris focused his attention on Vivi.

And her gaze was fixed on him. His heart twinged again. The urge to rip open the door and ask her to stay with him was strong, but what would they do, even if she agreed? They were both minors and he didn't make enough to support them, and he was pretty sure his parents wouldn't approve of him trying to override Vivi's parents' wishes.

So he forced the impulse back, and instead, placed his palm on the window, fingers splayed. Vivi hesitated, then placed her left hand—where her ring was back in place—on the glass matching his hand, mouthing, *Yo amo ti siempre.*

But would she? He couldn't bring himself to say anything, because despite that ring, nothing had been formalized. Arturo started the car, so Cris lowered his hand to his side and took a step back, even as the man put the car in gear and pulled away from the curb. Cris watched as it turned a corner and disappeared from view, taking what felt like his whole life with it.

The hardest thing was knowing this really was the last time he would ever see her. Especially if her dad had anything to do with it. Cris shut his eyes for the longest time, before glancing at the empty house where they'd spent more than one evening giggling on the porch as he kissed her goodbye. It was now just a shell. A house without a soul.

He nodded at it. "I know the feeling."

Stepping back to his old beat-up car, he put a hand on the hood, letting the residual heat from the engine warm it as he took one last look at the driveway, wondering who would park there next. It didn't matter, because it wouldn't be the Araya family. Then he got in his car and slowly drove away.

CHAPTER ONE

THE ROOM WAS awash with light from almost every angle to avoid having shadows from the team interfere with the surgical field. Viviani Araya should be used to being in an operating room. After all, she'd been a surgical nurse for the last fifteen years.

But not in Valparaiso.

It wasn't the first time she'd dealt with heartache in this place. And now, on the heels of a painful breakup, it had seemed natural to run here. She thought the town she thought of as home would nurture her and help her heal. Instead, she was being inundated with memories of a different time. Memories of sitting in the back seat of a car and crying her heart out.

Estevan had made her cry too. But now she was older and wiser, right? If she could survive the pain of a youthful love that never had a chance to grow, she could survive this. She just needed to give it time.

"Forceps."

She went stock-still, her breath stalled in her lungs. *Dios*. No! There was no way on earth fate could be that cruel. But that low gravelly voice—one that had once washed over her and made her shiver in the dark— she would know it anywhere.

Time seemed to move in slow motion. There were so many hospitals and clinics in her home city—how could she have wound up in the same medical facility as the ghost from her past?

Dark eyes met hers and his frown made her swallow. She wasn't wrong. It was him.

"Forceps." He repeated his request. And while his voice may have still been soft, she dared not mistake that for a softening in his attitude. He was angry at her hesitation in handing over the instrument he needed. She quickly found the right one and placed it in his gloved hand. The second she did, he stiffened and his gaze swung to her face, scouring the part of it that he could see for several long seconds. He said something under his breath and a muscle worked in his jaw.

He *knew*. Knew it was her. Knew she was back where they'd first met almost twenty years ago.

But he said nothing, just turned back to his patient and resumed the surgery—no faltering, no pause—as he moved on to the next step. A knee replacement was undoubtedly a very routine procedure for him. It was probably like driving home at night: it became a series of muscle memory stops and turns that required very little conscious input. It should be the same for her, but it wasn't. Not when Cris was standing just a few feet away. She'd been running late on her first day at the new hospital and had skidded onto the floor and was told where to scrub in and which room she needed to be in. She hadn't even looked to see if there was a board that listed the patient or the surgeon.

She'd just been desperate to get away from Santiago and hadn't cared where in Valparaiso she landed. She did now, though.

Maybe it was better that she hadn't known that Cris was doing this surgery. She might not have come into the room at all. Might have backed away from her old life and its heartaches.

Not that her present life was any happier.

Cris bit off the name of another instrument and this time she didn't pause or fumble. She deftly placed it in his outstretched hand, doing her best to ignore the electrical current that traveled along her fingers and up her arm as she did so. He was married. Or so she'd heard from a friend who'd since moved away. She hadn't been keeping track of him. At least not anymore. It had been too painful to hear that his parents had died in an automobile crash only a year after she'd left the city. But it was inevitable that friends had shared tidbits of information, although that rarely happened anymore. They had all moved on with their lives. Vivi included.

So why was the presence of a childhood romance now crowding her thoughts with memories that should have died long ago? It wasn't like she'd joined a convent. She'd had a few romances since then, including almost marrying Estevan. But Cris…

He. Was. Married.

So stop it, Vivi!

He must be as horrified as she was that they would meet up again.

Or maybe he didn't care. *She* shouldn't care.

Somehow she got through the next hour with no more missteps, and Cris basically ignored her. So maybe things were going to be okay after all.

Okay. Ha! Somehow she doubted she was going to get off that easily.

"Closing the site." That low voice rumbled over her again as he carefully placed a series of staples along the skin with a precision that sent a flash of heat over her.

She could always go somewhere else.

Really? A swear word slid to her lips, and she had to press them together to prevent it from escaping. How many times was she going to run from things that were uncomfortable? It seemed to have become the norm for her, recently. Actually, it wasn't just recently. She tended to shy away from people when they got too close. And those romances she'd thought of earlier were pretty short-lived, really. Except for Estevan, who had somehow worked his way into her life with a stubborn resolution that had made her laugh. Before she had time to take a few breaths, they were engaged. And that had proved a mistake because he'd evidently worked his way into someone else's heart with the same insistence that he had hers.

It was only after she'd had time to reflect that she realized he was probably more in love with the process of wooing a woman than he was with the woman herself. He'd probably done it more than once. But not with her. Not again. She'd ignored his texts, finally blocking him from her life altogether.

Which is how she'd wound up back in Valparaiso.

Valley of Paradise. Valpo for short.

It had been once. Paradise. A very long time ago. Something she needed to put from her mind. Because if Estevan had taught her anything, it was that she'd been right about not letting men get too close. She wouldn't make that mistake again.

"Good work, team. Our patient won't play soccer again after his injury, but he'll be able to coach or mentor, which is hopefully what he'll decide to do."

She hadn't realized their patient was an athlete, although she had thought he'd seemed awfully young to need a knee replacement. That was hard: having your whole life change in the blink of an eye and being unable to ever go back. Hadn't that been what had happened to her? First with Cris, then with Estevan? Her parents had urged her to stay in Santiago after her breakup, but she'd been adamant that she needed a change. And so, here she was. With a change she neither expected nor wanted.

Busying herself with organizing her trays

while the patient's anesthesia was reversed, all she wanted to do was get out of the room before she had to speak to Cris again. She needed time to gather her thoughts. Thankfully, once he was assured that his patient was awake and starting to communicate, he stepped out of the room. Her muscles went slack and she stood there without moving, pulling down some deep breaths before forcing her mind back to the job at hand.

The time went by fast and soon she had things separated and in order, and the patient had been whisked away. A new team arrived to clean and sanitize the operating room and get it ready for another patient so she stopped to discard her scrub gear in the trash bin, reaching to check that her hair was still secure in its twist. Then she slid through the double doors and glanced to the right at the nurses' station, hoping that was also the way to the staff lounge. She could really use a coffee right now—the stronger the better—since she hadn't had time to unpack her French press. She would have gotten to Valpo a week ago, but a car repair and severe weather had delayed her arrival. She barely made it in last night after nightmare traffic had turned what was normally a two-hour drive into seven.

She started to head toward the main desk, noting the board that listed the surgeries. She needed to find out the other ones she'd need to scrub in for today. Her eyes closed for a second; she hoped those surgeries would not include Cristóbal.

"Vivi, wait."

Santa Maria. Not now. Not when she was still trying to get over the shock of standing next to him. She needed time to process what had happened. Both with Estevan and her discovery that Cris was still in Valparaiso.

She slowly turned and found a man where once had stood a boy. Everything except those intense dark eyes had been covered by surgical gear a few minutes ago, and what she could see now blew her away. His lanky runner's frame had filled out in the best possible way, but the shock of dark hair still curled in every direction and was just as mouthwateringly sexy as it had always been. It would have been so much easier if he had lost most of his hair. But would it? Really?

Besides, fate couldn't be that kind. In fact, fate had been kind of a bitch over the last several weeks.

She tried on a fake smile. "Hi! I didn't

know you were at Valpo Memorial. At least not until I saw you in the operating room."

That dark gaze stared her down for a minute or two. "Didn't you?"

His words took her aback and she frowned. "I'm not sure what you mean by that."

"Surely my name was on the list of hospital staff when you came here looking for a job."

He made it sound like she'd been desperate or something.

"Actually, I didn't 'come here looking for a job.' I saw a posting at the hospital where I was *already working* as a scrub nurse and applied. I didn't scour the website looking for familiar names." She threw in another remark. "Besides, I might not have even recognized your name if I'd seen it."

That was a mistake, and he knew it because one side of his mouth curved. "Oh, really? I got a few letters that seemed to indicate otherwise."

Yes, she had written several long pages of prose that reiterated what she'd said the last time she saw him…that she would love him forever. That she would never ever forget him.

Her face heated. "I was a child back then." And she didn't talk about the fact that he hadn't written her back because she didn't want him to know how soul-crushing it had been that he hadn't cared enough to respond.

The way she'd never responded to Estevan's texts? No. That was not the same. She was convinced that he'd never really loved her—or he wouldn't have been able to jump into another relationship so quickly. It seemed she was forever doomed to love men more than they loved her. But not anymore.

"It seems we both were." His face turned serious. "And now we're both adults, so I assume we can both work at the same hospital—the same *quirófano*—without it causing a problem, correct?"

The inflection he'd given to the term "operating room" gave it an intimacy that made her wonder if she really would be able to function working that closely with him. But she had to, or had to pretend he had no effect on her. At least until it became a reality. They really had been kids the last time she'd been here. She neither wanted nor needed to stand around mooning after him. Since he was married, he'd obviously moved on as well. She was glad for him. And honestly, she was glad for herself. He was safely off-limits—even if there had been any temptation. Not that there was.

TINA BECKETT   21

"*Absolutamente*. It will be no problem."
And she meant it.

"That's good to hear. Because I just checked
the scheduling and it seems we'll be working
quite a few surgeries together, since one of
our other scrub nurses retired a few weeks
ago."

He'd looked to see if they'd be doing more
surgeries together? So maybe *she* wasn't the
only one who was going to have problems.
Maybe he was too. Except she'd already tried
to peer at the schedule board from a distance.
She just hadn't been able to read it. And it
sounded like he'd looked ahead at the procedures that were on the calendar and not just
on the white board. That could always change,
though, if she wound up stuck in an emergency surgery with another surgeon when one
of Cris's patients was due to be operated on.

But how often was that likely to happen?
She could at least hope it ended up being more
than the norm, though, couldn't she?

She tilted her chin. "I'm ready for anything."

He gave her a cryptic look, then nodded and
turned to go in the opposite direction.

She couldn't help but watch him go, and
even though his frame had filled out a bit, he

still had that lanky runner's walk that she'd always found so endearingly sexy.

She sighed. This was going to be hard—and honestly that was a good thing, since it meant she would be on guard—but if she had to work with him, maybe it was better that their first meeting had happened the way that it had—in an operating room full of people. Because having it come as a complete shock was better than having fretted over it during the weeks leading up to the move. That would have been worse. So much worse. She probably would have changed her mind about coming to Valpo Memorial.

But at least she would have been prepared. He disappeared around a corner, and she let muscles that she hadn't known were tight relax a bit.

Well, she really was prepared for anything now.

Right?

Cris shook his head as he sat in his office chair and stared at nothing. The shock of seeing her had thrown him into a tailspin, and it shouldn't have. What they'd once had was child's play compared to what life had thrown at him since Vivi's family had moved away.

His parents' deaths, his uncle's help getting through medical school, finally finding love again at the age of thirty, the three-year struggle to have a child, then his wife's cancer diagnosis that left him a single dad raising his beautiful daughter alone.

Yes, Vivi had written to him for almost six months after they'd left, but he hadn't had the heart to write back. It had felt kinder to rip off the Band-Aid and let them both heal and to let her form new connections, since her dad had mentioned maybe going back to the States after their assignment in Santiago. And she hadn't come back to Valparaiso after graduating from high school, so it had seemed Cris's decision had been the right one. Besides, he'd been grieving the deaths of his parents a year after they parted ways.

It had taken a while for Cris to move on with his life, but he had, and he'd hoped she had too.

So why had her return affected him the way it had? He'd lost his focus for several minutes while operating on Roni Saraia, which was not like him. At all. The thought had run through his mind that she had come back on purpose after all these years, which was ludicrous. He'd practically accused her of doing so, in fact. He groaned aloud. That hadn't been a proud moment.

It was obvious she hadn't known he was at the hospital before applying for the position, which was a relief. Because they couldn't take up where they'd left off. Not that he thought she wanted to. Nor did he. He had Gabi to think of nowadays. At five years old, she was impressionable and attached easily to people like her teachers and friends, so he had kept his love life simple and uncomplicated. It wasn't ideal. But it worked. And he had no intention of changing the way he did things.

His aunt and uncle were always willing to watch her on the rare occasions he went out on a date with someone, and he had never brought anyone to the house—even when Gabi wasn't there. And Cris wouldn't for a few more years until his daughter was better able to understand that people wouldn't always be permanent fixtures in her life…a lesson he didn't want her to learn for quite a while. His late wife had been estranged from her own parents—who'd been abusive—so there weren't even grandparents in the picture.

He was grateful for his aunt and uncle who'd stepped up to the plate and had been there for both him and his daughter, taking on the role of grandparents, since they had no children of their own. And although he'd been eighteen when his parents had died, they'd brought Cris into their home while he did his undergraduate work, and for most of his time as a medical student. Then he'd rented an apartment they had in the city up until he and Lidia had married. He wasn't sure what he would have done without them. He might not be where he was today without their help and he never let himself forget that.

He sighed and forced himself to look at the paperwork that was waiting to be completed, and then he still had rounds to do, including looking in on Roni to make sure the former soccer star was doing okay. He couldn't afford to spend a half hour every day hashing over things of the past, so he'd better learn how to deal with Vivi's presence in Valparaiso. Soon. Or his work was going to start suffering and that was something he was never going to let happen. Nor would he let it affect his family life.

Finally settling in his chair to catch up on paperwork, he put Vivi from his mind.

"How are you feeling?" Cris caught up with Roni the next day as the young soccer star sat in a wheelchair in physical therapy. The therapist was demonstrating how to do an exercise, but the athlete just sat there and did nothing, acting like he hadn't even seen her. Cris cocked his head at the staff member in an unspoken question and she shook her head to say no. That she hadn't gotten anywhere yet.

"Can you give us a few minutes?" he asked.

"Sure. I'll go see if we have some resistance bands for my next patient." Undoubtedly she already knew the answer to that question, but she was giving them some space like Cris had asked.

Once she was out of earshot, Cris sat in the chair she'd vacated and didn't say anything for a few seconds, just took in the hopelessness he saw in the man's face. A hopelessness he remembered well after his parents passed away.

"Talk to me, Roni." After a catastrophic injury to his knee that had required a complete replacement—an attempted repair at another medical center had failed—it was possible he could still run on the limb, but not at the same level as before. And putting that much stress on a new joint was never a good idea. Especially since it had been dicey getting things to work with what was left of his femur.

"Soccer is—*was*—my life. What will I do now?"

"You're going to take it one day at a time. But you have to try. Otherwise that surgery might as well have never happened."

"Maybe it shouldn't have. Maybe the other surgery would have eventually worked."

This was the hard part. Telling the patient a truth they didn't want to hear. "A portion of the bone had lost blood flow and was dead. If you hadn't had surgery yesterday, things could have been much worse."

"I don't see how."

"You could have faced amputation."

Roni went pale as he stared at him, the pain in his eyes going beyond physical discomfort. "Didn't I already? The part of my life that I loved the most was taken away from me. Isn't that a form of amputation?"

He was right. It was. Just like when Vivi and his parents had been taken from him. Like when Lidia had died. But those were things no one could change. And Roni's leg wasn't going to be restored to normal, no matter how long he sat in that chair and did nothing.

Had Cris's life ever been restored to normal? No. But he'd learned ways to move forward. Had learned how to wall off portions of himself in an effort to avoid the pain of additional loss. Not that that was something he wanted Roni to do. He was young and deserved to be happy. And he still could. If he could just get past this hurdle—which was a big one.

"You're a legend. Is this the way you want that story to end? With you sitting in this room day after day, refusing to try? Giving up? Is that the message you want to send to kids who idolize you? Who want to be just like you?"

"I'll soon be forgotten."

"And you will be if you just sit here. It's up to you to make sure that doesn't happen. You can still give back to the game. You can help other kids who have little or nothing—like you did—make their dreams come true."

"How? I can't play anymore."

"Maybe not. But you know what it's like to play the game. You know exactly how it *feels* to kick that ball past the goalie and rack up those points. The exhilaration that comes with it. You can share that knowledge with others."

"I don't know…" But Cris thought there might be a touch less resignation in his look than there had been moments earlier. The orthopedist had never played soccer, but he did know what it felt like to mourn what could never be brought back. And yet he'd somehow made a life for himself—a good one—even though he no longer remembered exactly when or how that decision had been made. He hoped Roni would get to that point as well.

And maybe Cris could help make that happen. "Listen, I can't promise anything, but I can look into camps for boys and girls who want to play and see how you can connect with them. Not just soccer but basketball and other areas. Or maybe we could have some kind of 'meeting of the minds' happen here at the hospital with experts from several sports weighing in. You could be involved with the soccer aspect. But only if you're willing to put in the work on your own recovery."

The man shrugged. "I can't promise anything either. But I'll try."

The PT specialist had come back, resistance bands in hand, and overheard that last phrase. "That's good to hear. So if you're ready, how about we get down to work."

Cris held out a hand and Roni shook it. "Well, I'll let you two get to it. I'll check in on you again before I leave for the day. I'm hoping we can release you tomorrow. You have a way to get back and forth to your PT sessions?"

"I do."

"Good. Think about what I said, and I'll see you later then."

They said their goodbyes and he headed to the glass door, blinking when he saw a familiar face just on the other side. Vivi. Great. Just what he needed. Taking a deep breath, he headed for her.

CHAPTER TWO

"How's he doing?" Vivi had come down to check on Roni, and she wasn't even sure why. She wasn't his doctor. She was just a nurse who'd scrubbed in on his surgery. But she still cared, and at her last job she'd often checked in on patients and no one had seemed to mind. But it might be different at Valpo Memorial. Besides, she had an idea and wanted to run it by Cris. But maybe she should do that in a place where they couldn't be overheard.

"I assume you're talking about Roni?"

She bit her lip. Was he about to chew her out? "I am. Is that a problem?"

"Not as far as I'm concerned. You're a nurse and worked on his case. I think he'll like knowing members of his team care about him. It might even help motivate him into doing his PT."

The last sentence slipped by almost unheard, because of what he'd said just before that. He considered her a member of the team? Something about that phrase made a warmth settle in her chest. She hadn't felt like she'd earned her place on that team yet, but he was evidently not going to hold their past against her. Although why would he? It hadn't been her decision to move away—it was her parents. Except she'd heard her dad say something about her being too young to be in a relationship and that their new assignment would help take care of that. Had her father asked to be moved because of Cris? Whatever his reasons it had worked. Her letters to Cris had gone unanswered. Just thinking about that made her squirm in embarrassment, imagining him telling his wife about the lovesick girl who'd written long missives that promised things that were impossible. She wished she'd been more like him back then, able to let things go that she couldn't change. Well, she might not have been strong enough to do that twenty years ago, but she was now. There was no going back, and she had no desire to.

"He's resisting doing his therapy?"

Cris glanced over at where the physical therapist was standing with a walker. "I think it's part of the grieving process. His career has been a huge part of his identity. Trying to shift gears from the past isn't always easy, but it is necessary."

Her head whipped around to look at him, but the surgeon was still looking over at Roni. There was no way he'd been talking about their childhood romance. Besides, he was married and that would be inappropriate.

"Well, I'll go over there and say hello," she said.

"Let me know if he starts doing some work."

"I will." She gave him a smile that she hoped looked friendly but not too friendly, noticing that he didn't wear a wedding ring. Lots of surgeons didn't, though. They would have to be taken off every time they scrubbed in and then put back on. It got to be a huge pain. If she were married, she doubted she would wear her ring to work either. For some reason that simple little ring he'd given her came to mind. She shoved the thought back into its sealed compartment.

Just because he didn't have one on didn't mean anything. And unless he'd divorced in the intervening years, he was still unavailable. Actually, even if he had divorced, she'd do well to steer clear of any romances here at work or anywhere else. Estevan had showed her all the reasons why that was a terrible idea.

Walking over to Roni, she noted he was still seated. The smile she gave the PT was genuine as was the one she gave the patient. "Hi, Señor Saraia. I know that Dr. Diaz was just here, but I wanted to check on you as well and you weren't in your room. I figured you might be down here."

The nurses dealt with wound-dressing and checking on vitals anyway, so she wasn't out of order in coming. But after what Cris had said, a glimmer of worry had appeared about their patient's state of mind. If she ever couldn't do her job, it would rock her world as well. Maybe not to the same extent, since her whole identity wasn't wrapped up in her job, but it would still be hard.

He looked slightly peeved at having yet another medical person pestering him, so she held her hand out to the therapist. "Hi, I'm new here. Viviani Araya. I'm one of the nurses on the surgical floor."

"Bella Trasseti. Nice to meet you. Roni and I were just getting ready to do some walking on his new knee, isn't that right? Isn't that what you told Dr. Diaz?"

As if caught red-handed, the man made a

sound that sounded like exasperation, but then nodded. "I guess I need to keep my promise to him."

Bella moved the walker a step or two closer, holding it steady as Roni grasped the handles and then hefted himself up on his good leg.

"You're allowed to put weight on your injured leg, and I won't have you do anything that might damage all of Dr. Diaz's hard work, okay?"

Roni nodded, but his jaw was tight, a muscle jerking in his cheek. Vivi wasn't sure if it was due to pain or concentration or a mixture of both. When he glanced around the large open room, which was bustling with other patients and PT staff, she realized what it might be. He was embarrassed to be caught barely able to walk and there were quite a few patients who were glancing their way, probably recognizing their celebrity patient.

She knew a tiny bit about what he was experiencing. Hadn't the looks of pity at her other hospital made her want to melt into the woodwork? Her fiancé had been a surgeon she'd worked with on occasion; it was how they'd struck up a friendship that had turned into more. And the aftermath of finding out he'd been secretly romancing another nurse hadn't been fun. Her friend in Human Resources reminded her that she'd tried to tell her she was headed down a slippery path, but Vivi had been so sure that it wouldn't happen to her. And yet it had. Hopefully she'd learned her lesson.

"Do you mind if I pull a couple of those rolling partitions over here?"

Bella tilted her head and then her eyes widened in understanding. "No, go ahead."

It actually would work perfectly, since Bella's cubicle area was in the far corner of the room. Even blocking the view from the door would probably help. So she pulled two of the devices over and unfolded them so that together they made an eight-foot wall.

Roni sighed. "Thanks. I didn't think having people watch me would bother me—I should be used to it, right? But this..." He motioned down at the dressing on his leg.

The physical therapist gave his shoulder a squeeze. "You need to tell me when you feel uncomfortable, so we can find a way to fix it. I'm glad Viviani thought of it."

"So am I." The look he gave her was one of gratitude with a little something mixed in. Something that made her pause.

No. She was imagining it. This was a man

with legions of fans. And probably plenty of women to boot.

He did as Bella directed, slowly making his way to the end of the partition before turning a big half circle and coming back the other way. By the time he got back to his seat his arms were visibly shaking. "*Mierda!* Why do I feel so damn weak? It shouldn't be this hard to just walk."

"Yes, it should," Bella said. "You've just had major surgery. It's not just the injury. It's the aftereffects of anesthesia, which hang on for a while—not to mention the body's attempts at healing use a lot of energy. Give yourself a little bit of grace."

"Grace. Maybe my body should give me a little bit of that and cooperate."

Vivi started to touch his arm before thinking better of it. "Bella is right. It takes time. You'll be surprised at how fast you'll bounce back. Muscle memory will kick in and you'll be on your way."

"On my way to what? Sitting on the sidelines watching the sport I love being played out in front of me?"

She understood that he felt helpless about what was happening to him. Powerless to stop it. But letting himself linger too long in those thoughts was just going to make him sink deeper and deeper. It was like a quicksand. If you ventured too close, you'd have trouble extricating yourself from it. If anyone knew that, she did.

Before she could say anything, though, Bella did what she'd been afraid to do and touched his hand. "You'll do a lot more than sit on the sidelines. For our next session, you're going to help me brainstorm a list of things you can do using your knowledge and experience in the sport."

"It's going to be a mighty short list."

"You might be surprised. Now, that's all the torture I'll put you through, since it's our first session, but don't expect me to be so soft on our next go-around."

He gave the first real smile Vivi had seen. Then he said, "Spoken like a true coach."

"Hmm… I've been called a drill sergeant before, but never a coach. I think I kind of like that." She pulled his wheelchair over. "Why don't you hop into your ride and if Viviani doesn't mind, I'll have her go with you back to your room."

"I don't mind at all." But when she went to help him, Bella stopped her with a slight shake of her head. Ahh, she wanted him to do it on his own. Her nurse mentality was to help her patients whenever she could. A PT's mentality was to let a patient do all he or she could on their own.

So she stood by as Roni awkwardly tried to figure out how to hold onto the chair and turn to get into it. Bella did offer guidance on how to shift himself so that he didn't twist his bad knee. Then he lowered himself into it, slumping forward and blowing out a loud breath.

Bella smiled at him. "It'll come. Don't dwell on the hard stuff. Just tackle each step as it comes and celebrate what you can do, rather than getting stuck in what you still need to accomplish. Getting ahead of yourself won't do you any good and could just cause strain in a different part of your body."

He made a snorting sound that might have been agreement or might have just been an indication that he was withholding judgment.

At any rate, Vivi got behind him and asked if he was ready, to which he nodded. "More than ready. But thank you, Bella."

She was a little surprised to hear him thank the woman who'd caused him to work so hard. But he had. Vivi hoped that was a good sign.

"You're welcome. I'll see you back tomorrow and the next day and the one after that, until we have you working independently."

"I guess I have no choice in the matter?"

Bella wrinkled her nose and said, "None at all. Take him away, Viviani."

With that, she turned the chair and headed toward the door.

Cris glanced up from a sheaf of messages when a knock sounded at his door. Leaning back in his chair, he tried to figure out if there was an appointment he'd forgotten. "Come in."

Vivi poked her head around the corner. "Are you busy?"

Not someone he was hoping to see. But here she was, and he was fairly certain she wouldn't have come if it wasn't something important, and he had asked her to check in after she'd visited their patient. "Nothing that can't wait. Come in. Is it about Roni?"

She made her way to a chair, and he waited for her to sit down. "Yes and no. Yes, he completed therapy and seemed to have a better mindset by the end of it."

"That's good. And the other part?"

"Well, it's still kind of about Roni, but it's also about the hospital. I assume this department sees their share of athletes walk through the doors, and some of them probably are in the same situation as Roni—not knowing what the future might hold."

"You would be correct."

She seemed to hesitate. "I know I just got here and haven't earned the right to throw out ideas, but I feel like I have to. What if the hospital had someone like Roni on staff, whether as a volunteer or a paid position, if Valpo Memorial doesn't already do that? He's a recognizable face to most athletes and could talk about career-changing injuries and what helped him make it through."

"Except he's not through it himself."

"Yes, but if he saw that once he was on the track to recovery there was a path opened for him to help others, it might give him something to look forward to. Might give him the incentive to do the work that needs to be done."

He sat back. Her idea kind of went along with his own thoughts, only it took things a step further. In a good way. There was a problem, though. "And if Roni thinks we're just trying to capitalize on his name for the hospital's financial gain?"

"If we aren't blasting his name on social

media or using it in advertising campaigns, then I don't think he'll see it that way. He could even give lectures to coaches or professionals in the medical field on how to motivate athletes who become patients. You just admitted there are quite a few of them."

Cris glanced at his watch. "What time do you get off work?"

"I'm actually off right now."

"I have the rest of these messages to get through and I need to make a phone call. But if you're free, can we discuss it a little more over some cafeteria food? I skipped lunch and I'm starting to feel it."

"Oh…um, sure. I don't have plans."

She didn't sound exactly thrilled and he wasn't either, but having her in his office like this with the door closed was beginning to have an effect on him. One he didn't want. And the phone call he needed to make was to his aunt to make sure that she could watch Gabi for a couple more hours. He had no doubt she would be thrilled to. But he was also conscious of the fact that he never wanted to presume. It wouldn't be fair to her or to Gabi.

Why not just make the call with Vivi present? He wasn't sure, and he didn't want to examine the reasons too closely. He was pretty sure she'd heard about his marriage from classmates, although why would she have? He hadn't kept up with where she was or what she was doing.

"If you have plans or would rather discuss it during working hours, I'll completely understand." He hoped she knew that things between them needed to remain on a professional level. So again, why not call his aunt and uncle about Gabi right now?

For that exact same reason. The less they knew about each other's personal lives the better. It was why he'd never answered her letters or kept up communication with her as they went on with their lives. They couldn't be friends without those emotions being dredged up. At least he couldn't. Their romance had needed to stay in the past, and that couldn't have happened if they'd pined away for each other. It still needed to stay in the past. And it was up to him to make sure he followed that rule.

"No, it's not that. No plans. I just don't want to interfere with your home life."

Home life. Did she already know he had a child? Well, if she did, she did.

"No, you won't. So I'll meet you in the cafeteria in, say, fifteen minutes?"

"That's fine, I'll see you down there."

She turned on her heel and exited his office, leaving him to try to get his mind back where it needed to be. He took care of his messages and then locked his office before heading for the elevator and making his call to his aunt.

She answered on the first ring, just as the elevator doors opened on the first floor. The cafeteria was just down the hallway and he saw Vivi waiting in front of it, but she was facing the other way, so he kept his voice low but kept walking. "Aunt Pat, I'm running a little late at work and wondered if you could keep Gabi for another hour or two."

He wasn't sure what he would do if that didn't work for her. He gave an internal shrug. He would just have to cancel and they could discuss whatever idea she had on a different day.

"Oh, are you going into surgery?"

"No, just some unfinished business." He frowned. It was true in the strictest sense, but why had he worded it that way?

"Oh, good," his aunt said. "That's fine. We were headed out to do a little shopping anyway and had to drive by the hospital, so

Gabi insisted we come by. We're just coming through the front doors. Are you in your office?"

He'd just reached Vivi and stopped to stand beside her, hurrying to finish the conversation while mouthing "Sorry" to her.

"No, I'm actually down in the..." Things seemed to happen in slow motion as he heard a familiar squeal and automatically turned toward the sound. Just in time to spot a small figure launching herself down the hallway toward him, her aunt calling out to her. He glanced back at Vivi and saw that she had also spotted the pair too and turned to look. Her eyes met his and he could almost see the understanding dawn on her face, although she was still a good hundred feet away.

He broke his gaze and knelt down to greet his daughter, opening his arms. When she crashed against his chest, he closed them again, holding her tight. "Hi, *querida*. Did you miss me?"

"Yes." Small hands patted his face, and a surge of pure love enveloped him. In the midst of his heartache over Lidia's death, Gabi had been the one thing that kept him going. And with her energy and zest for new adventures, his daughter could run circles around him.

Pat caught up with him. "Gabi, you can't just run off like that. Sorry, Cris. She doesn't normally leave my side."

"I know that." He smiled up at his aunt to show her that he wasn't worried about any of that. "She just saw me and wanted to say hi. Where are you guys headed?"

"The *centro comercial* just down the road."

He reached for his wallet. "Let me give you some money for food or a snack."

"Not a chance. I have money. She got an attendance award in school and so we're celebrating."

Cris glanced over to where Vivi had been, knowing he needed to introduce her. But the spot where she was standing was now empty. Had she left? Or just gone inside to give them some privacy?

Turning his attention back to his daughter he smiled, letting her wiggle out of his hug. "Attendance award, huh? That's a pretty big deal."

"Yeah! School is fun! Except for Matias Cabral. He's mean. Maria even says so."

He assumed Matias and Maria were classmates. "Did you try being nice to Matias?"

"No. Because he's *mean.*"

Cris couldn't contain his smile. There was

no arguing with that kind of logic, and he had no idea if the boy really was mean or if he was just looking for attention, like many other children in that age bracket. "Well, try being nice and see what happens."

"Okay." It was said with a slump of her shoulders, but he had no doubt that Gabi would indeed try to show kindness. If there was a problem with Matias being a bully, he was pretty sure her teacher was already on top of it. She'd been one of his patients a year ago when she needed knee replacement surgery at age sixty. She'd been teaching for a long time and said she loved her job. He believed her when she said she didn't plan on retiring anytime soon.

Gabi went back over and stood beside Pat. "Can we go, Ti-Tia? I'm getting hungry."

Cris's aunt laughed. "You're always hungry. I have no idea where you put all the food you eat."

"In my belly," his daughter said, as if it should be obvious to everyone.

He rose to his feet. "Well, then, you'd better go get something to put in that belly. And I have a meeting to go to. I'll see you in an hour or so?"

"Better give us three," Pat said. "Just in case we find something interesting."

He wasn't sure where he would be if it weren't for his aunt and uncle. Oh, he would have gotten by, but he would have had to hire a nanny or a sitter. And though he knew people did that every day with good results, he was glad Gabi could stay with family. When he'd broached the subject of bringing someone else into the equation as a way to give the couple a little more time to nurture their own relationship, they'd acted hurt and so he hadn't mentioned it again. He had made them promise to tell him if they couldn't watch her for whatever reason. They had, but so far had always seemed thrilled to spend time with her.

So he said goodbye then and promised he'd see them soon. How easily the words slipped from his tongue, even though no one ever knew if they could keep that promise. Shaking those thoughts from his head, he waited for them to disappear from sight before giving a sigh and heading into the cafeteria, hoping there wasn't going to be a need for an in-depth explanation about Gabi or worse, about Lidia or what had happened to her.

He frowned when he went in and saw her

sitting at a table with nothing in front of her. Then he realized that there were no workers in the normally busy place, except for one lone person who was restocking the napkin holders on the tables. When he glanced at his watch, he saw that it was after six. He couldn't remember exactly when they closed, but it must have been recently.

He headed over to her. "I'm sorry. I didn't realize they wouldn't be open."

"It's okay. And it looked like you were busy. If you need to go be with your family, I'll understand." Her voice sounded strained somehow.

"My aunt is going to watch her for a while. They just stopped in to say hi before they headed out on a shopping trip."

"Your aunt?"

He frowned. "Yes." Ahh, he got it. His aunt looked much younger than her sixty-one years, and he could see how Vivi might have mistaken her for Gabi's mom. There was nothing to it but to tell her the truth, because if he let it hang, things might get even more awkward than they already were. And it would feel like he was lying, even though he hadn't been the one giving her that idea "Gabi's mom…my wife...died about a year after our daughter was born."

Her eyes widened. "Oh, Cris, I'm sorry. I didn't realize. I'd heard from Paulette that you were married years ago, but I didn't know she'd passed."

They'd undergone fertility treatments in order to have Gabi, and although the doctors had tried to reassure him that it had probably not played a role in her ovarian cancer, he'd had a hard time believing that and had carried a load of guilt that he still hadn't completely shed.

"It's been a while. Gabi doesn't even remember her." Why had he even added that last part? It was true, but saying the words sent pain through his midsection just like it did whenever his daughter asked to see pictures of her mother. Fortunately, his wife had thought to make a video for Gabi as a way for her daughter to get to know her. She'd taped birthday wishes for her first ten birthdays, all she'd had time for before she became too sick to do any more. They were now through half of the tapings and when they came to the end of the messages, Cris knew it would be hard. It would be like losing her all over again.

"I can't even imagine." She stood and

touched his hand before dropping her own by her side.

He frowned. "Sometimes I can't either. It hasn't been easy. But Pat and Guilherme have always been there for me and Gabi."

"I'm glad." She tilted her head and studied his face. "Do you want to meet another time? I'll completely understand, if so."

"No, I'd still like to, if you have the time. We'll just need to do it somewhere other than the cafeteria. Do you have any favorite places to eat?"

"Here in Valparaiso? I haven't been here in so long, that I really don't. I'm fine with anything really. Even just *pastel de choclo*."

The iconic Chilean dish consisted of corn puree, basil, ground beef and a few other ingredients. It was simple and filling and there were few people in the country who didn't eat it on occasion.

"I know a place that makes a lot of comfort-style foods. And it's just around the corner, so we won't need to drive."

"Sounds perfect. Let's go." She slung the strap of her small purse over her head so that it hung diagonally across her chest and waited for him to lead the way.

CHAPTER THREE

HE WASN'T MARRIED. At least not to a living person. Not anymore. But that didn't mean he wasn't married to her memory.

That reality floated through her head over and over again—random thoughts. *Dios!* The safety net she thought she'd had with Cris being married had just been yanked from beneath her. But it shouldn't matter. And it wouldn't. He wasn't divorced, hadn't chosen to leave the relationship like Estevan had— his wife had died. And they'd been very much in love. She thought she'd seen a glimpse of that in his face as he talked about her—even though he hadn't really said much, other than the fact that it had been hard.

And like she'd thought a few moments ago: it shouldn't matter. And it didn't. She wasn't getting involved with another coworker. And definitely wasn't getting involved with some-one from her past. Both paths would lead to heartache—she knew that from experience. She'd rather not repeat the same mistakes. She was older and wiser now. And she was going to be a hell of a lot more careful about where she let her heart venture. She was going to keep it close, like a pet dog that might bolt the first time she let it off its leash.

They turned the corner and, *gracias a Dios*, Cris was right. The restaurant was close. Nestled among the vibrantly colored buildings that Valpo was known for was a mint green bistro that had a scattering of white wrought-iron tables and chairs on the cobbled area out front. It didn't take long for a hostess to find them a spot at the outer band of seating. She gratefully sank into a chair, just realizing how tired she was after the long day at the medical center. It was a shame that they couldn't just sit here and enjoy some tapas and knock back a few drinks while watching the sun set over the city. But they wouldn't even be here if it weren't for her "idea." And she was a little hesitant to really go any further in-depth about it. Especially now that they were off hospital grounds.

What if he ended up thinking it was a ridiculous idea?

A waiter came over to the table, and to hell

with it, she was ordering wine of some type. Maybe it would give her some courage. Plus they'd walked to the cafe, so it wasn't like she had to drive anywhere right away. And by the time they made it back to the hospital, she'd be back to normal, right?

"I'd like a Melvin, please." The nickname for *melón con vino*—a popular drink in Chile— the Melvin was their version of the Spanish sangria. Only instead of red wine, Chileans used white wine, adding it to honeydew melon. It was absolutely delicious and refreshing. Especially in the heat of the Chilean summer.

"Would you like that for one or to share?" The server looked pointedly from one to the other.

Dios! She hadn't even thought about that. A lot of times *melón con vino* was a communal drink, served in a hollowed-out melon with multiple straws and passed around for everyone to enjoy. "Just for one, please. One straw," she added as if that wasn't already a given.

Her face was so hot it must be flaming red. There was still something about Cris that made her forget where she was. It was still the shock of seeing him again after all these years. She would get over it in a few days.

"Can you bring a pitcher?" Cris said. "I haven't had a Melvin in ages."

Leave it to him to save the day. Like the time that she'd skidded up the driveway, almost late for curfew after they'd spent hours at a stream after school. Her dad had been furious, but Cris had diffused the situation by saying they'd had a school project to do. It wasn't true—they'd been making out—but it had kept her from getting into trouble.

The waiter left to get their drinks and she tried to lighten up what had almost been an embarrassing situation. "I would have taken you for a dark ale kind of guy."

"Me? No. I hate beer, actually, even though I know it's expected at sporting events. I don't drink much, for the most part."

That surprised her, for some reason. But should it have? They'd been so young when they were dating that they hadn't had a chance to learn what either one of them would be like as adults. The fact was, they really didn't know much about each other anymore. They were essentially strangers. And as angry as she'd been at her dad for dragging her away from Valparaiso, looking back, she could see that he really had been looking out for her welfare. If they'd stayed, it was very probable that she and Cris would have married right out of high school. Who knew if either of them would be where they were professionally if that had happened?

But they could certainly enjoy a drink together now without messing up either of their futures. And without the effects of teenage hormones entering the picture.

The waiter brought the spiked fruity beverage in a clear glass pitcher, complete with chunks of melon, and two goblets, each with its own straw. She smiled. At least the server had asked and not assumed, or that could have been a tricky situation.

She kept her order simple, just bread slathered with a healthy amount of mashed avocado. She'd never understood how the pairing could be so delicious but it was, which was why it was so ubiquitous in Chile. Cris ended up being the one who ordered a hamburger. When she raised a brow at him, he smiled, igniting that pesky dimple in the side of his face, one of the first things she'd noticed about him when they'd met all those years ago.

"What?" he asked. "You made me want one."

He'd once made her want a lot of things,

none of which she'd gotten when they'd been younger. Cris had wanted to wait. She had not.

It was probably one of her biggest regrets about their time together. Because for years afterwards, she'd fantasized about what it would have been like to sleep with him. But again, it made the transition a little easier because sex had not been tied to her memory of him.

"I guess I was in the mood for green today."

When he looked quizzically at her, she motioned to the pitcher of Melvin and mentioned the food she'd ordered.

"Ahh, I guess you were."

She ignored the fact that he was in a dark green polo shirt. Because that was one thing she wasn't getting. Not in the past and not now.

"Is your aunt keeping your daughter overnight?" Too late, she realized how that might have sounded and hurried to add, "I didn't know if that was something your daughter enjoyed. I remembered liking having sleepovers with friends."

"She does, but it doesn't happen as often as she might like, since I like having her at home at night."

Vivi could understand why. His wife had

died and a natural reaction to that might be that he was protective of his daughter and his time with her.

She took a sip of her drink and sighed as the sweet liquid hit her tongue. "I don't think I could ever get tired of this drink. It's the perfect summer cooler."

The waiter came out with their food and set it in front of them before moving on to a different table.

Cris picked up his burger, then glanced at her. "So tell me more about this idea you had."

That's right. This wasn't a normal outing. She'd asked for this. "You mentioned that quite a few athletes come through the ortho department. Do you have any idea what the statistics are?"

He seemed to think for a moment. "Probably about fifty percent. We're known for treating sports injuries."

"And how many of those injuries are career-ending?"

There was a longer pause. "I don't actually know. Some patients follow back up with us and some don't."

"I can see how that might happen." She took a bite of her sandwich. "Roni seemed pretty despondent after getting the news that he'd never play soccer at the same level again. Like I mentioned earlier—what if we had someone like him on staff who could help patients work through the various emotions that go along with that kind of a diagnosis?"

He flipped the lid off his burger and took off the pickles, setting them to the side. Another thing she didn't know about him.

"Like a therapist?"

"Not a licensed one, no, since I'm sure the hospital already has someone like that on staff. I'm talking about someone who's actually faced the hard decisions that those patients will face and has a list of resources available or someone who'll just sit and listen and share what's worked for them."

"Got it." He seemed to mull over what she'd said for a few minutes. "I think that's a good idea. And you mentioned Roni might be a good fit."

"I think so. I don't know if he'll go for it or not. But it sure would have helped if he'd had another athlete to talk to. Instead, he got doctors, nurses and PT specialists who probably don't have the foggiest notion what it's like to have to change careers because of an injury."

"True." He took a bite of his food and there was a pause while he swallowed. "But he hasn't even worked through his emotions yet, much less be expected to help anyone else with theirs."

"I get it. But he will be in a month or two. I expect him to start shifting his focus as he heals. He'll be looking for something to replace soccer with. Maybe it'll be coaching, or even sportscasting. But maybe those options will be too painful right now. Not every injured athlete wants a daily reminder of what they can no longer do."

Cris nodded. "I like it. Can you research whether there are centers who are already doing what you're suggesting? They might have some tips on who to look for and what to bill them as. Meaning outside consultants or actual hospital employees."

"Do I need to run it by the administrator before I do any of that?"

"I don't think so. Not yet. Not until we have something concrete to go to him with." He smiled. "And I'll let you broach the subject to Roni and see if that is even something he'd be interested in. I suspect he'll want to give it some thought, since there's no way it will pay as high as what he's getting now. Or as coaching."

"And I should probably see how he handles

PT. But even if it's not Roni, I think the idea could still do some good. Maybe a past patient who's looking for a way to give back."

"I would agree. I'm surprised one of our team hasn't already thought of it." He looked at her for several seconds. "I wasn't sure how I felt about your showing up at the hospital. But it looks like you might do all of us—including Roni—a lot of good. Thanks for speaking up."

She laughed. "If you hadn't listened, I might have gone over your head."

When his smile died, she was quick to cover his hand with hers. "I was kidding."

He pursed his lips. "Actually I hope you never feel that you can't go to someone else. I'm not always the biggest advocate for change, since I tend to be a creature of habit. It sometimes takes me a while to get to where I need to be."

She couldn't imagine him losing both his parents and his spouse, even though the events happened years apart. Hadn't she thought that he'd probably be protective of his daughter? And he'd admitted that he had a hard time with change, maybe also as a reaction to what he'd been through. She finished her drink, then poured another one. She held up the pitcher in silent question and he shook his head no. "I need to drive home from the hospital. And like I said, I rarely drink."

Yes, he had said that. Hopefully he didn't think she was fond of being tipsy. She wasn't. Using a clean knife, she fished out a couple of pieces of melon from the pitcher and added them to her glass. That would be her dessert.

She finished the last of her avocado toast and dabbed her mouth with the napkin.

When Cris pushed back from the table, she thought for a second that he was going to leave, but instead, he just laid an ankle on top of his knee. "So where are you staying?"

"Right now? A bed-and-breakfast, since I just got into town. I need to look for a place. I was planning on contacting a realtor this afternoon."

"My aunt Pat is a realtor. I could ask her to check around, if you'd like. Do you have a specific area in mind?"

It surprised her that he would offer. But at least finding a realtor would be one thing off her list. "Something close to the hospital would be great. I'd love to be able to walk to and from work. Do you think she would mind? I know rentals aren't always the most lucrative."

He smiled again, and she stared at his face while trying to appear nonchalant. How was it that the man was a thousand times more good-looking than she'd remembered?

"Actually, she manages quite a few properties and has some rentals of her own. She likes being in the business and helping people. They both helped me a lot after my parents died."

A pang went through her. How lucky she was that her parents were alive and well.

"Thanks, then. I don't really have a preference, other than distance to the hospital. A two-bedroom might be nice in case my parents decide to visit."

At that, Cris's jaw tightened up, although his smile didn't fade this time. "I'll have her get in contact with you. Can I have your number?"

She gave it to him and then said, "She can call me or text. Either is fine."

The waiter came with their check. When she started to ask him if he could divide their orders into separate bills, Cris had already taken it and handed the man his credit card. As if reading her thoughts, he murmured, "I'll put it on my expense account since we were talking business."

So he'd already been expecting to pay. But this was a lot more expensive than the hospital cafeteria would have been. "Let me at least pay for the *melón con vino*. I can't imagine they'll want to shell out for alcoholic drinks."

"I'm pretty sure they do it all the time. And I've put them on my expense reports when going out with other surgeons to brainstorm."

Even though he rarely drank? Well, she wasn't going to argue with him. "Okay, if you're sure. But if there's a problem, please let me know."

"I will. But there won't be. Will you talk to Roni soon?"

"Are you okay with that? You said you wanted me to do some research first."

He nodded. "I do, but even if there's not a precedent for doing like you'd suggested, maybe we'll be the first hospital to adopt something like this. Let me know what he says."

"Do you want to be there to hear it in person?"

He glanced at his watch and then got to his feet and waited for her to follow suit. "No. I trust you."

She looked outside and realized it had gotten dark. How long had they been here, anyway? She certainly hadn't meant to monopolize his entire evening. It had gone by fast, and that made her uneasy. And now they still had to walk back to the hospital.

But, when they stepped outside, the lights were beautiful and there was a warm breeze blowing. The familiarity of the city she called home washed over her in a wave and she had to stop for a minute. Santiago had been beautiful too, but this was just…home.

"Are you okay?"

She nodded, blinking back sudden moisture. "I'd forgotten, that's all. It's just so damned gorgeous."

He turned toward her, looking into her face. His hand rose as if he was going to touch her before he let his arm drop back to his side. "Yes. It is." A long moment went by and a tingly sensation rose up inside of her. The last time he'd looked at her like this, he'd…

Cris took a step back, ending the intimate moment with a suddenness that made her lightheaded. Or maybe that was the wine. Whichever it was, she stiffened her backbone and forced a smile. "Sorry for the maudlin sentimentality. It's just been a long time since I've been here."

"I get it. I'm not sure I could ever leave the city."

She could understand that for sure. His feelings about the city had to be tangled up with those he'd lost. Staying here would make him feel close to them.

And that look he'd given her? There was no way he'd been about to kiss her. That would be ludicrous. What they'd had had been childish and fleeting. Nothing like marrying someone and then living life with them. Having a child with them. And it made her feel more alone than she'd felt in her whole life. Even more than when her fiancé had walked away from her to be with another woman.

"Shall we go?"

They walked in silence and the beauty of her surroundings had ceased to captivate her. All she wanted right now was to get back to her hotel and hibernate for the night. Hopefully she'd feel better about things tomorrow. Actually she'd felt fine during dinner. She'd enjoyed his company and the conversation. It was only afterwards that her own thoughts had spoiled things.

But things always seemed worse at night. At least that's what people said, right? Tomorrow would be another day.

It took ten minutes to get back to the hospital, and when they got to the doors, he started inside, but she didn't. "I'm headed home."

"Are you driving?"

"Yes, my car is here—why?"

"You were drinking. Let me take you."

She tried to assess her faculties, but she was smart enough to know that she probably wasn't the best judge of that. But she'd only had two drinks.

"Come on, Vivi. It's dark and you're no longer as familiar with the landscape like you once were." And there was something in Cris's eyes that had gone hard, and she had a feeling if she tried to argue her point he was going to lose respect for her. But why? She knew she wasn't drunk. Not by a long shot. But what she'd thought moments earlier was still true.

"Okay. I can take a taxi to work in the morning. Thanks."

The hard look softened. "Good. Which hotel?"

"Esquina da Val. Actually, the name is written in English, Val's Corner, 'cause the owner's name is Valeria and her house is on a corner." She giggled and then put a hand over her mouth, shocked by the sound. Maybe the alcohol had hit her a little harder than she'd expected.

"I see." The side of his mouth flicked up for a quick second.

Dios. The man was more than gorgeous. Getting in a car with him was probably more of a colossal mistake than eating with him had been.

Except it wasn't. He'd thought her idea had merit, so that made it worth it. And her muddled feelings had to be because of the alcohol, even though it didn't normally affect her. She'd been thirsty, though, and had downed the first glass fairly quickly and then had eaten most of the wine-soaked melon chunks after she'd finished the second. She gave an internal groan.

He was right about her not driving.

"I'll bring my car around. Wait here."

Two minutes later, he drove up in a sleek, sporty-looking SUV. She was sober enough to realize that it was an expensive vehicle. He got out and opened her door, and she climbed in.

Within minutes they were on one of the roads leading from the hospital, heading up a hill, past one of the city's funiculars, which were much needed due to the steep terrain.

Thankfully she didn't need to use any of them to get to Val's Corner, although the place was on a hill.

"I think I know where the place is, but if you can remember which street it's on, that would be a huge help."

"It's on Gaeta." Somehow she remembered the name, even though she'd only been there once.

A short time later, he pulled up in front of the pink building. It was a good thing, because she'd almost fallen asleep in his car.

"Thank you. And thanks for letting me discuss my thoughts on adding a staff member for our athletes."

"Not a problem. Let me know what you turn up once you look into it. And if Roni seems to be in favor of helping with it."

"I will." She got out and slammed the door behind her and headed for the gate.

Val's Corner had a cobblestone sidewalk leading up to a path of the same material. It ended at the front door, a huge wooden affair that had an intercom. She buzzed the door and let Val know it was her. Her suitcase was still on the bed. She should unpack, butut that might need to wait until tomorrow. She was suddenly exhausted, both physically and mentally, and quite honestly, emotionally as well.

A clunking sound let her know that the door's lock had been released, so she went in and headed up the stairs to her room, one of three on the second floor. And she was as surprised this time as she was the first time she'd set foot in the place. Her room had its own bathroom rather than a shared one on the hallway and was as spacious as her bedroom had been in her childhood home. And that was saying a lot, because her house had been one of the larger ones in the city, since her dad was a diplomat.

She set her suitcases on the ground and then went to the overstuffed chair that sat in one corner and dropped into it with a sigh. Then she pulled out her phone and texted her parents, letting them know that she was settled in and that work had gone well. The one thing she'd left out was a biggie, and that was that she was working with Cris. Although she wondered if her parents would even remember who he was. Her dad might, though. He'd been unhappy with her choice of boyfriends, since Cris's family had definitely not been from the same part of town as her family had, although they hadn't been poor.

None of which mattered now.

She pressed Send and then curled up in the chair and leaned her head back against the cushion. Today seemed so unreal. Who would have ever thought she'd dine with an old high school flame? Certainly not her.

But she was pretty sure she was going to wake up tomorrow and find her situation unchanged.

One thing that would be changed, though, was her attitude. She'd be over the shock of seeing him again. Of hearing his voice. Of having him look at her. And she'd be able to regain control of a situation that had almost spun out of her grasp today. And no more drinking around him.

Or wondering what might have been.

Tomorrow she was going to slip into a part she needed to learn how to play. A part she should have been playing her whole adult life. That of a colleague who never ventured beyond the boundaries set before her. She'd seen what could happen when she colored outside the lines. And there would be no more of that. Not with Cris or any other work acquaintance. It would be strictly business.

She'd come here to push a work romance into the past, where it would stay. And then she was going to look toward the future and embrace all that it could be.

And Cris wasn't part of that future. Nor would he ever be.

She was going to remember that and stick to it. Even if the going got tough.

CHAPTER FOUR

CRIS SHOVED HIS unruly hair out of his face as he turned a corner and continued his run. The Quinta Vergara park had always been his locale of choice when it came to getting out of the gym and into the real world. Running on a treadmill was one thing, but stepping onto a real road surface with a variety of surfaces was another. And so far, even today, it hadn't disappointed him, even if he was sweating a whole lot more than he would have in the climate-controlled space inside the gym.

The parallel between running and life didn't escape him. The difference between the controlled atmosphere of the hospital, with its sterile environment and mostly predictable events, was at odds with life outside those walls. He'd gotten an up close and personal reminder of that fact two nights ago when he'd gone out to dinner on business and it ended up being a whole lot more personal than he'd planned for. At least on his part.

He turned a corner and stepped off a dirt pathway and onto a concrete sidewalk, feeling the change and how his body automatically adjusted to it. Why hadn't he been able to do that when he and Vivi had stepped outside the restaurant into an evening filled with stars, rustling leaves and hushed voices? Maybe because of the obvious emotion in her voice when she'd looked up and gazed at the sights and sounds of the evening and murmured at how she'd forgotten.

Cris, on the other hand, had forgotten nothing. The instantaneous attraction he'd always felt when she was near. The beautiful tilt of her smile. The painful edge of seeing tears on her lashes.

He'd almost tilted her head up for a kiss. Had almost lost sight of why they'd been in that restaurant. What if Lidia had still been alive? Would he have lost his head then too?

No. He'd loved Lidia deeply. But their relationship had been different. Comfortable. They'd been from the same world, both born and raised their whole lives in Valpo. Being with her had felt so natural. They'd been happy and fulfilled and he was never going to forget that.

He would have remained faithful to her no matter what. But she wasn't here as a talisman to ward off danger. She was gone and no matter how much he might wish otherwise, she wasn't coming back.

And so when he'd stood there with Vivi, the past had come rushing back. The carefree impulsive love of youth. It had arrived out of nowhere and almost overtaken him.

He pushed himself harder, made his muscles work for each step, showing them this wasn't some game. He wasn't a carefree teenager anymore. He was an adult with adult responsibilities. He was a single dad doing the best he could to raise a daughter. To be father and mother to her. The thought of her being hurt because he couldn't control his libido was an unacceptable trade-off. He might have lived through the reality of losing Vivi when he was a teenager. He'd also lived through the wrenching pain of Lidia's death. But that didn't mean he couldn't do his damnedest to protect Gabi from the pain of loss. Loss didn't always come through death. It also came by choice or by circumstances.

So if he could prevent her becoming attached to someone who might or might not stay, he could prevent the pain that came if that person did, in fact, leave. Or worse.

The burning pain in his thighs reminded him that he wasn't out here running as a form of self-flagellation. He slowed his pace to a more tolerable level. But were his thoughts any better? Wasn't he punishing himself for something that hadn't even happened? Cris hadn't kissed her, no matter how tempted he'd been. He'd stopped. Had pulled himself back from the brink. And now that he knew what could happen, he would be on guard.

And really, he didn't know the Vivi of the here and now. He only knew the childhood version of her. If he could remind himself of that and that any feelings he might have were generated out of distorted memories of what they'd once had, he should be able to avoid a repeat.

It hadn't helped that Gabi had asked later about the pretty *señora* she'd seen him standing next to at the hospital. He'd given her a vague answer about her being a new nurse, but the look in his aunt's eyes said she'd recognized Vivi and knew exactly what she'd once meant to her only nephew. Worse, when she'd dropped Gabi off that night, she'd apologized for bringing her to work and said in a low voice meant for his ears only that she hadn't realized Vivi was back in town.

He'd been honest and said he hadn't known it either until they stood across from each other in the operating room.

She asked if he was okay with her being here.

It was a question he hadn't been able to answer then and one he still couldn't answer now. It had certainly been easier before her arrival.

He slowed to a walk, putting his hands behind his head as he went through his cooldown routine. He'd only seen Vivi in passing the last two days, since he did most of his surgeries on Wednesdays and Thursdays, unless it was an emergency surgery like Roni's had been. And she hadn't contacted him about whether or not she'd done the research he'd asked or whether she'd spoken to Roni, who had been released from the hospital and was coming to PT on an outpatient basis. He was due to see the athlete in his office again on Friday of the current week. Hopefully his patient was in a better frame of mind.

And hopefully by that time, Cris would also be in a better frame of mind and sticking to his plan of not socializing with Vivi outside of office hours. Next time the cafeteria was closed, there would be no going off campus to discuss anything. And there definitely would be no alcohol involved. Because when he'd thought she was going to drive, a surge of anger had come over him. Alcohol and driving did not mix. No one knew that better than he did. And he took great care to make sure he put no one at risk. Including his daughter.

Gabi was number one in his life and that's the way things needed to stay. At least until she was old enough to understand that bad things sometimes happened. And at five years of age, he hoped she was a few years away from needing to know that.

He got back to his car and took a towel out of his gym bag, dragging it across his face and arms and then tossing it back. Glancing at his watch, he grimaced. He'd taken longer with his run than he'd meant to, so he didn't have time to go home. Thankfully he had a change of clothes back at the hospital and would shower there in the bathroom that adjoined his office.

And then he would start his day.

Vivi was in at the nurses' station when *he* got off the elevator. Looking like a bronzed

Adonis in gym shorts and a T-shirt that clung to his form in a way that should be illegal, he'd obviously been working out.

And he's off-limits, Viv. At least to you.

But that didn't mean she couldn't admire the hair that hung almost to his chin in decadent curls. That was one thing that hadn't changed about him. He'd always worn his hair a little longer than was conventional and let it be a little wilder.

It had driven her wild as a teenager, just like it had all the girls. She'd always been in awe that he'd chosen her out of countless others who would have loved to be with him.

But that was then and this was now.

His dark eyes met hers for a second longer than necessary before veering away in the direction of his office. Where he obviously was headed to shower. And her mental reminder leaped off a cliff and vanished.

Her eyes closed in an attempt to block the images that were now pounding at her lids demanding admittance.

Please, no.

"He's a hunk, isn't he?"

Her eyes jerked back open, horrified at being caught. Then she realized the comment wasn't aimed at her. It was between the two other nurses at the desk. She blew out a breath in relief and pretended to be doing some paperwork that was so engrossing that she couldn't possibly have heard what they were talking about.

"What do you think, Viviani?"

She glanced over, blinking. "Oh. About what?"

The other nurse chortled. "Never mind. If you'd seen it, you would know."

Oh, she'd seen it all right.

Vivi gave a half shrug as if she were totally confused. But it served as a wake-up call. What if word got back to one or both of them that she and Cris had a history? How would that possibly happen? She was pretty sure he wasn't going to say anything, and Vivi definitely wasn't going to. So she just had to make sure no one saw her making eyes at him or seeking him out. Or going out to eat with him again. Which she had no intention of doing.

Except she did need to talk to him about what she'd found out about other hospitals employing athletes or having programs similar to the one she was talking about. There were none in the area. Theirs would be the first. She wasn't sure if that was going to be a plus or a minus as far as that went.

She just needed to find a way and a time to go talk to him. And that time definitely wasn't now. But what she could do was text him. Or send an email to his hospital mailbox. Once she talked to Roni, which she still hadn't done. But she had gone down to PT and talked to Bella, since she was still handling his case. She said that Roni was still going through the stages of grieving and hadn't completely given up hope on returning to the field as a player.

He was going to eventually have to come to terms with it or risk wrecking all the work that Cris had done on that knee. She'd smiled and asked if she could come down during his next session. The physical therapist was thrilled. "He seemed to really connect with you, so I think it would do him good to see you."

And that session was today at three this afternoon, so she had a while. A few minutes later, Cris came out dressed in fresh clothes, an iPad in his hand. He looked straight at her. "Can I see you about our athletic patient?"

She played dumb, even though both of the nurses from earlier had gone to treat patients. "Athletic patient?"

He threw her a look which made her cringe.

She wasn't very good at acting clueless. So she'd better get up and moving before anyone came back and saw her talking to him. "I'll be over in just a minute."

"Okay." He headed back to his office.

Dios! She at least needed to tell someone where she'd be. If it looked like she'd disappeared from the desk, someone might want to know where she was, especially since she was so new to the hospital. So she headed to the patients' rooms and found Dora on the first try.

"I need to go consult with one of the doctors about a patient. Are you good?"

"Yep, go."

She assumed that happened quite often here, just like it had at her previous hospital. There were all kinds of reasons. Medication changes, scheduling changes and so on. It was normally just taken at face value, and Dora didn't ask which doctor needed her, which was a relief. "Just page me if you need me, but I shouldn't be long."

"It's not Dandalia, is it?"

She had no idea who that even was. "No. Why—is he or she long-winded?"

"He. And the longest. Okay, see you."

With that, Vivi headed back down the hallway, dread filling her as her steps took her ever closer to the man's office. When she was there, she hesitated before knocking.

"Come in."

She did as directed, almost falling over herself to get to one of the two chairs that were parked in front of his desk. "You wanted to see me?"

"Yes, any information on what we talked about?"

He made it sound almost clandestine. And that was the last thing she wanted: to feel like they had some kind of secret between them. Well, they did, kind of. But this wasn't from twenty years ago.

His hair was still damp from his shower and the room was filled with the warm scent of some kind of wood. Cedar, maybe?

She tried to ignore it. "I did call all the area hospitals that might have some kind of program but struck out. As far as I can tell, they have mental health specialists on staff but nothing other than that." She went on before he could ask. "I was going to text you. I did go talk to the PT here at the hospital about how Roni is doing and it sounds like he's still in denial. But he has a session today at three. I plan on going down then."

"He has an appointment with me on Friday as well. If today doesn't pan out, maybe you can come to the appointment."

"Which is at what time?"

Cris checked his electronic device. "Eleven. Are you scheduled for surgery on Wednesday or Thursday?"

"Both days."

He didn't say anything to that, and since they were both procedures that he was involved with, she tried to read his body language, but if he cared one way or the other, he wasn't showing it. "Will you let me know what Roni says today?"

"Do you want me to actually ask if he would be interested in helping with a program like the one I mentioned?"

"Yes. Don't make him any promises but ask if it's something he could see himself doing— helping other athletes who find themselves in his position."

"Got it. But I have to tell you…if I get there and feel like it will hurt his session or his chances of recovery, I'll hold off. I'd rather say nothing than do more harm than good."

"We're in agreement there." He looked at her, then said, "About the other night."

Heavens. What on earth could he want to

say about that? That he was disappointed in her for letting the booze go to her head?

"What about it?"

"I'm sorry if I made you uncomfortable. We should have probably sat somewhere at the hospital and talked."

He hadn't made her uncomfortable. In fact, she was pretty sure he was the one who felt uncomfortable about what had happened. "It was fine. But you're probably right. We should stick to the hospital grounds for work-related subjects."

He looked at her a little closer. "And those are the only subjects we should be talking about."

Ahh, so he was warning her off. Well, there was no need for it. She'd done plenty of warning herself off when it came to that. Especially after the comments made by Dora and Elena. "I agree. We can just act like we didn't know each other before I came to work at the hospital."

"I didn't mean that. Eventually someone is going to know and say something about our past. It'll make it worse if people think we lied about it. Because they'd start wondering why."

"I'm pretty sure no one is going to be interested in my past."

But they might be interested in his. Actually, she was pretty sure they would be. But it would be easier if they just thought of him in terms of a man who had lost his beloved wife.

"Have you never worked in a hospital before? People want to know everything about everything. Even if it's none of their business."

She laughed. "True."

He paused. "I've always liked your laugh."

"And this is related to hospital business how?" But she didn't stop smiling. Because she couldn't. And he'd just showed her that the task of keeping to impersonal subjects might be harder for him than he made it sound. Because no matter what else had transpired in her life, she would always have a soft spot when it came to him. That whole first love thing. How could she not allow those good memories to sometimes overshadow the present? And she hoped that he might still have at least a memory or two that he cherished about her.

He'd been married, and she'd been almost married, and yet they did have history. Nothing would take that away no matter how much they didn't want the past to bleed over to the present.

"It's not related to business. But it is the truth."

"Well, as long as we're talking about truth—I still like your hair. I'm glad you never completely cut it off." When they were together, his hair had been almost down to his shoulders.

"I've thought about it. Many times. But Lidia…" He shook his head. "Sorry. None of that matters."

His wife had liked his hair too. Somehow, the thought of him finding someone else— rather than being painful—brought comfort. And she was sad that he'd lost what they'd had. Vivi had thought she'd found love as well. Only to find that the universe evidently didn't have that in store for her. At least not with Estevan. And not with Cris, either.

"I'm sorry she's not here for you now." She wasn't sure why she'd said that, but it was true.

"Thanks. Me too. I'm sad she won't be here to see Gabi grow up."

"I think maybe somehow she can. At least I'd like to think so."

He smiled. "I'd like to think so too." He stood. "Anyway, I won't keep you. But thanks for checking into the other area hospital thing and for trying to feel Roni out about the program."

"He might respond better if it came from you, since you're his surgeon."

Cris seemed to think about that for a minute. "I don't think he believed me completely when I told him he'd never play soccer on the same level again. That his repaired knee would not be able to handle the stress of pro soccer."

"Well, I'll try. But don't expect him to jump up and down over the prospect."

"No. And he won't make nearly as much from a hospital job as he would from advertising endorsements. People will recognize him for a long time to come. He could still make a lot of money."

She didn't think that's the route he would go, though, and she couldn't put her finger on why she thought that. "I don't think he's about the money, honestly. I know a lot of these athletes are, but I think Roni truly loves the game. He never once mentioned money to me. Not about losing his income or anything else like that."

"No, me either. Which is why he may opt to coach. It would keep him in the game. And if that's what he wants to do, then more power to him. But I would still like to see what we can do for the future Ronis that come through our doors."

"Me too. Okay, I better go. How hush-hush do you want all of this?"

"For right now? Until we've talked to the hospital administrator about it, I'd like it to stay pretty much between us. I don't want him to think we're going behind his back with anything. And as soon as you talk to Roni today, I'd like us to go together to talk to the powers that be about it."

She could understand that. "Do you think the administrator will go for it?"

"Marcos is a pretty big soccer fan himself. I can see him finding an angle that helps the hospital raise funds. He's good at the money side of things, which might make it tricky, since I don't want Roni to think this is just a fundraising tactic. But I also think he'll be interested in doing the right thing for the athletes themselves."

Vivi hadn't met the man yet, but since there was a staff meeting next week for all new hospital employees, she would meet him then, if not before. "I'm fine if you want to present it to him on your own."

"It was your idea. I want you there. You'll be the one who can present it to him with passion."

She wasn't really sure about that, but she did understand Cris not wanting to try to talk about it on his own. And she did have some thoughts on how to kick-start this thing and get the word out there. And it would have the side benefit of attracting some of the top players, who would come to them for treatment if they knew that Roni endorsed the hospital.

"Okay, as soon as I see Roni today, I'll try to feel him out. And I'll let you know."

"Sounds good. And like I said, regardless of how this plays out with him, I'd still like to present the program to Marcos. Are you okay if I set up a time with him?"

"Sure. That's fine."

"Okay. Talk soon."

With that she left the office, wondering how good of an idea it was for them to "talk soon." Because they'd been talking a whole lot more than she envisioned when she saw him on the other side of that hospital bed and realized he was the top orthopedic surgeon in the hospital and quite probably the city. She'd been determined to avoid him if at all humanly possible. And now all of a sudden they were brainstorming an idea that she'd come up with. So instead of avoiding him, she'd just committed herself to seeing a whole lot more of him.

And she wasn't sure what she thought of that.

But one thing that she was pretty sure was going to haunt her long into the night was the fact that he still liked her laugh.

She kept replaying those words in her head. It was just an offhanded comment and meant nothing more than the words themselves. So why did she keep hearing so much more behind them?

She didn't know. But she'd better find a way to minimize that comment and anything else he might say in the future. Or she was setting herself up for a whole lot of heartache. Maybe even worse than what Estevan had handed her. Because it would mean she was turning her sights toward a man she couldn't have back when she was a teenager and for a man she still couldn't have today. Whether it was the whole rebound thing or not, it wasn't healthy. And she, for one, was not about to let herself go there.

* * *

Roni's face turned red and Vivi flinched, waiting for him to flambé her for even thinking that the great Ronaldo Saraia would deign to be assigned to giving pep talks.

"You want me to head up a program at the hospital for injured athletes?"

"Well, we need to run it by the hospital administrator, first. But basically, yes."

He looked at her as if she were crazy. "Why do you think they would listen to me?"

"Are you kidding? You're every kid's fantasy for the future. You pulled yourself up from nothing and played your heart out each and every game. They'll listen."

His brows went up. "Okay. I'll think about it. I have some folks I'd need to talk it over with to make sure it wouldn't affect my brand. Because even if I'm never able to play again, I still love the game and want to support it in any way that I can."

Wow, his attitude had done some shifting over the past several days and she was glad to see it. Before, he'd been afraid his "brand" was going to disappear off the face of the earth if he couldn't play. And now he seemed to be moving past that kind of thinking.

"I get that completely. And we don't want to do anything that will hurt your ability to do that either. I just know you could do a lot of good for the individual athletes who make up soccer. They're just as important as the game itself, don't you think? Without them—without *you*—there wouldn't even be a game. It's made up of individuals just like you."

"Wow, that's a lot of weight on my shoulders." Unexpectedly, Roni worked his way over to her, using his walker, and enveloped her in a big hug. "But thank you for everything."

"Hey, it's you I need to thank for even considering it."

When she looked up, her eyes going over his shoulder, she saw that Cris was in the doorway staring at them, and for some reason he didn't seem very happy. What was he doing here?

She pulled free and waved him over. "Here's Cris…er… Dr. Diaz now."

When he made it over to them, Roni reached out to shake his hand. "Vivi was telling me about the idea of starting an athletic support group."

Cris's eyes were on her, though, rather than

on the other man. "And what do you think about the idea? It's hers, you know."

"I figured that out almost immediately. And I think it's a great one. I told her I need to iron out some things before I can agree to help, but I think the folks in my camp will be happy that I'm still able to do something for soccer."

"We'd appreciate anything you can do. But now I have to steal Vivi away. We have an emergency coming in and I need her."

"An athlete?" Roni asked.

"No, not this time. I'll see you on Friday at our appointment?"

Roni nodded his head. "I'll be there." He shifted his glance to her. "And thank you. I mean that. I guess that means we'll be working together on this, if it all gets approved?"

"I don't know about that. It depends on what the administration wants the program to look like. But you're welcome." She wanted to be careful where he was concerned. Patients could easily become attached to their doctors or caregivers. And even if the whole patient/staff relationships thing wasn't forbidden, she wasn't interested in him that way and she didn't want him to get any ideas.

It had nothing to do with the strange look Cris had given her when he'd walked through that door. And speaking of Cris, he was already headed toward the door, and it was clear that he expected her to follow him. So she did, hoping that whatever emergency it was, it would have a good outcome. Because she could use some good news. Her phone pinged and she looked down at it, not recognizing the number. Then she went stiff. She didn't recognize the number but she recognized the first couple of words of the text, because she'd seen several of them before she'd left Santiago. It was from Estevan. And he wanted to talk.

Not happening. She pressed some buttons and blocked the new number, almost running into Cris as she did. She pulled herself back to allow some space to come between them and sighed. What could she and Estevan possibly have to talk about. When she had some time, she would sit down and compose a text that made it clear that they were done. That chapter of her life was closed. Just like the chapter between her and Cris was.

Closed. Forever.

Yes. She could definitely use something that had at least the possibility of a good outcome right about now. Crossing her fingers behind her back, she got onto the elevator with Cris.

CHAPTER FIVE

THEY SCRUBBED IN side by side without saying a word to each other. She still didn't understand what she assumed was a glare that he'd given her down in PT or the cold shoulder she'd gotten on the way back up to orthopedics. He'd told her that their patient—a fifteen-year-old female—had been injured in a car accident. She'd been going to celebrate her Fiesta de Quince when a drunk driver hit the side of her car. Her mom was killed instantly, and her dad had been severely injured as well. Clara had been left with a shattered femur that would need to be rebuilt.

It was a terrible tragedy. But when she'd said as much, Cris had shot her a look and said that the tragedy was that people still got behind the wheel of a car after having too much to drink.

Was it a commentary on how he'd had to drive her home after dinner the other night?

He was right to be angry about the accident. She was too. He'd just been so vehement about it.

He finished scrubbing in first and there was a nurse waiting to snap his gloves on. She did the same for Vivi.

When she arrived in the operating room, she went up to take her place at the instrument table and checked them over before glancing at the patient, who'd already been intubated and was ready to go. She had on heavy makeup, but there was blood spatter on her face—from her own injuries? From one of her parents? The fifteenth birthday ritual was such a big part of Latin American countries that the thought of something like this happening was heartbreaking. Clara would wake up in a different world from the one she'd just come from where she'd probably laughed as her hair and makeup were done, surrounded by friends and family.

Her mom was gone and her world shattered, just like her leg.

She pulled her thoughts back to the surgery at hand. None of those things could be changed. But they could help Clara regain the use of her leg.

She glanced up at Cris and it was déjà vu.

All she could see were his eyes. He was looking at her as well, and she couldn't tell if he was still angry or not. Although realistically if he was angry at her for some reason, they were going to have it out after the surgery, because she was not at fault here.

"Are you ready?" His voice wasn't hard anymore, though.

"Yes."

When they unwrapped the dressings that the EMTs had put in place, she could see that the actual injury was a mess. The part of the femur that was in one piece had perforated the skin and had been exposed to the air and all kinds of contaminants. Even as she looked, she spotted a dime-sized piece of bone stuck just inside the wound.

"Cris." She brought his attention to it, only realizing afterwards that she'd said his first name. But that probably wasn't an issue because a lot of doctors didn't stand on formality.

He nodded and retrieved the piece, dropping it into a jar of saline, the way they would do with any other pieces that were floating loose in the wound. They would piece together what they could and hope the bone would fill in what they couldn't. The piece he'd just dropped in the jar probably wouldn't be able to be reattached, but it was crucial that they clean out any fragments that could cause complications later on. Miraculously, there were no large severed vessels, but there was still a lot of blood.

"Scalpel." This time, she handed it over without the hesitation of that first surgery. He opened the wound further and began carefully flushing the wound to remove any debris, using forceps to pick out more bone fragments as they came to the surface.

He gave a running commentary both for the benefit of those in the room as well as for the recorder, which was in use for every surgery. "Displaced open fracture of the femur with multiple small fragments. Three main sections of bone that I can see."

He glanced around. "We're going to be here a while. Can someone check and see if we have the staff to scrub in as needed to relieve us in shifts?"

Someone left to do that, while the rest of the surgical team continued doing their jobs.

He finished flushing until he was satisfied that no foreign material was left in the wound and then set out to reconstruct what was left of her bone.

Three hours went by as Cris began forming a type of scaffolding that would hold the three main sections of bone in place while it hopefully healed, and then added in two other pieces that were large enough to screw into.

"Length looks to be good."

So there was still enough bone that the overall length would be close to what it was pre-accident. Which meant if all went well one of her legs wouldn't be noticeably shorter than the other. Where there had been one fragment in the glass jar when they started there were now seven. Fewer than Vivi thought there would be. And so far, she hadn't fumbled at all during this surgery. It gave her hope that she'd be able to maintain a professional demeanor even when things like that puzzling look he'd given her down in PT happened. She'd been trained for this and it was important that she be able make it through. If she ever felt patient care was going to suffer because of her personal life, then she needed to put in for a transfer or relocate, just like she'd done after discovering her fiancé had fallen in love with someone else.

Dios. She did not want to have to write Estevan back, but it looked like at this point that she had no choice. But it would be the last time. And if he contacted her again, she would change her own number.

Five hours after they had started, Cris finally seemed happy with the way the leg had been reconstructed. "I'm going to close up, starting with the inner sutures."

Even though he had to be mentally and physically exhausted after standing over the patient for so long—it had taken a couple of tries to get things fitted the way he wanted them to be—he continued on as if he still had plenty of energy. The tables and floor gave another story, though. They were littered with gauze and metal pieces— symbols of the hope of a leg that might heal.

Then he was done. "Let's wake her up."

The anesthesiologist gave a reversal agent and once he deemed she was ready, they extubated her and waited for her to stir. Cris went to the head of the table and talked in low soothing tones. "Clara, can you hear me?"

Her eyelids fluttered and then she looked up, obviously still in that confused fog that surrounded the anesthesia medication. The girl nodded and tried to say something but Cris put his hand on her forehead. "Don't try to talk yet. We're going to put you in a room and let you wake up a little bit more, then I'll come in and see you."

The girl nodded again, before letting her eyes slide shut.

"Wheel her down to recovery. I want to check her hemoglobin and make sure she won't need supplemental plasma. I'm going to check on her family."

Oh, God, that was right. Her mom was gone. And her dad? Were there any siblings?

Cris turned to the team, "Good job, everyone. That went as smoothly as it could have, and that's thanks to all of you." His eyes landed on her and then away before he headed out the door, leaving them to complete their tasks. This went much quicker than the surgery and everyone filed out, leaving the room to be thoroughly cleaned and disinfected for the next surgery.

She headed down to the cafeteria to get a coffee, even though she only had a half hour left of her shift. A surgery like that drained her, even though she wasn't the one who was performing the operation. She was pretty sure everyone on the team felt the same way.

She got her coffee and headed back out, her gaze tracking to the left for a second and spotting a familiar head of hair. It was just the back of him, but the slump of his shoulders and the way he was kind of hunched over as if in pain made her stop and head toward him. Rounding the table, she saw that the rest of him didn't look any better. He was pinching the bridge of his nose as if his head hurt and his eyes were closed.

"Cris, is everything okay?"

He opened his eyes, the brown irises so dark that they seemed almost black. "It's fine."

Before she could stop herself, she pulled out a chair and sat down. "No, it's not. Is it the patient?"

"No. She's fine. At least until she wakes up and realizes what happened."

"I know." Maybe that's all this was about, but she couldn't shake the feeling that there was more to it.

"It's just so senseless. Why would someone get behind the wheel of a car if they weren't fit to drive? Why wouldn't his friends stop him? Or whoever served him those drinks."

"Maybe he was drinking at home. With no one around to intervene."

"I know. And ultimately it boils down to being his responsibility and his alone. But, dammit, no one should have to go through what I…" He shook his head.

Her throat dried up. "Is that how your wife died?"

He blinked as if remembering she was there. "No. It was my parents. They were killed as they went to celebrate their twentieth wedding anniversary."

"By a drunk driver."

"Yes."

"I'm so sorry. I knew your parents had passed in an accident, but I didn't know the circumstances. Your comment about not drinking much. Is that why?"

"Yes."

If she remembered right, he didn't even finish his glass of Melvin. And there she'd been with no idea why he'd seemed so irritated with her for even considering driving. Her heart ached for all of the loss he'd experienced.

"You don't have any more surgeries today, do you?"

"None scheduled. But who knows what will come in next."

She put her hand over his. "Cris, you can't change the world or prevent people from doing things that hurt others no matter how much you may want that to happen."

Her fiancé had hurt her deeply by tossing her aside for someone else. She'd had no control of that or of what Estevan was doing now in repeatedly contacting her. Even her dad had hurt her deeply by tearing her away from all her friends and from Cris when he'd moved the family to Santiago. And even though she could see why now, it had changed the way she'd viewed her father for a long time afterwards. She'd thrown some terrible words at him, and even though she'd later apologized for them, they'd both done some things that they regretted.

"I know. But I wish to God I could change what that girl is going to go through as the realization hits her."

"What happened to the driver of the other vehicle?"

"He wasn't hurt at all."

She frowned. "But he was arrested, wasn't he?"

"Yes. From what I heard he was driving without a license. It seems he was a repeat offender so it had already been taken away. He'd been to jail, rehab—and still couldn't get his life turned around."

"Addiction is a terrible thing. I'm not excusing him. He should not have been behind a wheel and I truly hope he won't have access to alcohol for a long time to come."

"Me too." He gave a wan smile. "Roni is right. You are a pretty persuasive person."

"Come on. My shift is over, and my coworkers have already told me to go home. The last thing you need to do, though, is go home and dwell on what happened." Then a thought hit her. "Your daughter. Is she waiting for you?"

"No, she's with my aunt. I wasn't sure how long the surgery would take so she offered to keep her for the night."

So he really would be alone at home. After his announcement, Estevan had moved out of their apartment the next day while she'd been at the hospital. So she went home to a very different place. It had been a terrible feeling and one of her reasons for leaving Santiago and starting over.

But fate had a funny way of showing her that she'd never be truly free of her past. Things she'd thought were left behind came back to haunt her at the oddest times. And now here she was with Cris again after twenty years away. That wasn't to say that she hadn't thought of him over those years. She had. More than once.

He probably felt the same way about his parents' deaths and the death of his wife. They would never completely leave him. And that's how it should be.

"I know we said we'd keep this professional, but surely we can break that rule just this once. I promise not to pounce on you or anything."

One side of his mouth went up in that delicious smile of his. "As I remember it, no one pounced on anyone."

"All right—so there shouldn't be a problem, right?"

"Persuasive. Yes, you are." He sighed and slapped his hands on his knees. "But I really don't want to go home. What do you want to see?"

Ha! That was a loaded question and one she'd better not dig into too deeply. Because it might break the rule they'd just made. "One of my favorite places as a kid was the Cerro Alegre overlooking the bay. We would go up the funicular and find a restaurant that had a good view and enjoy it. But we don't have to eat. If I remember right, there's a sightseeing spot just as you get off the lift."

The funiculars of Valparaiso looked like odd train cars that traversed terrain too steep for a car or other forms of transportation. The ones that were still in operation were considered national treasures and were a top tourist destination. And the views at the top of those hills couldn't be beat.

"I took Gabi there once and she liked it. But I think the funicular was her favorite part of the whole excursion."

"I bet it was." The little girl was the spitting image of her father with her dark curls that fell over her eyes despite the little bands that had been used to try to hold those locks at bay.

"Okay, let's go. Do you need to change?"

Cris was already back in street clothes, but she still had her scrubs on. She took a sip of her coffee, which was now lukewarm, and made a face. "Yes. I have some clothes in my locker. I can meet you back here in say fifteen minutes."

"That sounds like a plan. I'll let my aunt know where we are. Oh, and I talked to her about your need for housing and she said she'd look into it and try to get a list together of available places in the next couple of days."

"Oh! Thank you. And please say thank you for me. See you in a bit."

As she was changing in the staff locker room area, she started having doubts about what she was about to do. But since it was her idea and she didn't want to have to explain what she was worried about, she'd just have to grit her teeth and bear it. The problem was that she was looking forward to the outing a little too much. And that gave her pause.

But surely she could get through this without any problems. She was an adult. She'd met plenty of men she found attractive and hadn't gone to bed with them. And even if she were willing, Cris promised to be on his best behavior. Well, not in those exact words but close enough.

She glanced in the mirror to see the worry on her face, though, and gave herself a mental lecture.

You are helping him get over a terrible memory. Nothing more, nothing less. Got it?

With that, she headed back down the elevator to meet him.

Cris leaned back in his chair, glad for the diversion. He hadn't been lying when he said he didn't want to go home. Although he wasn't

living in the same apartment where he and
Lidia had lived—he'd moved closer to his
aunt and uncle so that it would be more con-
venient to take Gabi back and forth—there
were still memories everywhere he looked.
Every picture of them together or of his parents was a reminder of his loss. Of all that his
daughter would miss out on. He was used to
it and most days it didn't bother him, but tonight?

Oh, yeah, tonight it would. Especially if he
didn't have his daughter's presence to help
distract him.

Vivi reappeared and she was now dressed
in a white gauzy skirt and navy blouse. A
silver bangle enclosed one slim wrist. She
looked very bohemian and matched the city's
vibe perfectly. And yet it was who she was. It
was what he remembered of Vivi from their
teenage years.

In reality, she was more beautiful with
tiny lines fanning from her eyes that spoke
of laughter and a happy life than she'd been
back then. And he was glad for her. Glad that
she'd been able to find joy in living. Cris's
joy came mainly in the form of his daughter and his work. And he frowned, realizing
he didn't have much of a life outside of those

two things anymore. So this trek up Cerro Alegre would be good for his...what did they call it? His soul? Although he wasn't so sure anymore that he had one of those. His ability to forgive seemed to come less and less easily nowadays.

He stood. "Ready?"

"As ready as I'll ever be."

The way she said that gave him pause. "You don't have to go, you know. I'm not going to go out and do anything crazy."

"Neither am I, so we're both good." But the nervous laugh that accompanied the words didn't make him any more confident in going along with her suggestion. But other than calling her a liar, he was going to have to take her at her word.

"So we're going to be sane and rational, then?"

Her laugh when it came this time was real and happy-sounding and made him smile.

"Since when have we ever been sane and rational when we were together?"

His smile widened, thinking of all the crazy stunts they'd pulled back then. "I don't regret any of it, though. Do you?"

"No, I don't. Not a minute of it." She held his gaze for a second before looking out the window at the gathering dusk. "But if we're going to do this, we'd better go now."

"Are you okay taking my car to the funicular?"

"Yes, since you probably know the way better than I do. It's going to take me a while before I relearn the city."

Before they relearned each other.

The thought came and went so quickly that he almost missed it. But as long as that relearning involved friendship, there was no harm in shared memories. Right?

Right.

They got in his car and despite the traffic of those heading out to various clubs and nighttime activities, the main rush hour was already finished. Various buildings had spotlights on them, highlighting the street art that Valparaiso was known for. He thought again that Vivi looked like she could have been born and raised in Chile despite spending her earliest years in the States. Maybe because her heart was Chilean, that blood handed down from her father. He almost snorted. A father who, although he bore the last name that announced his heritage, seemed almost embarrassed by that fact. Or maybe it had just been Cris, who hadn't grown up in the best part of town. But his parents had been hardworking individuals who loved him.

He shook himself free of his thoughts. And glanced over at her to find her staring out the window.

"I'd almost forgotten how much I love this city. I think it was home for me more than any other place I've ever lived."

"Santiago is nice too. It's a bigger city with more choices of things to do."

One of her shoulders flicked up in a half shrug. "It is, for sure. But I never really considered Santiago home. Although if my engagement had worked out, I probably would have stayed there."

She'd been engaged? He hadn't known that.

"I'm sorry for whatever happened."

"Me too. It wasn't the most pleasant breakup, but, like most things, it was for the best."

It made sense now. "That's why you came back to Valparaiso."

"Yes."

Hell, and he'd allowed himself to think that it might be because of him. That seemed so egotistical now. "It had to have been hard to leave your parents and all that you cared about."

Including her fiancé? He was pretty sure Vivi had never lacked for male attention. He'd even seen it in Roni and hated to admit that he'd felt a hint of jealousy over it. A jealousy he had no right to feel.

Vivi sighed. "I'm glad for the chance to start over, honestly."

Start over? He swallowed. Did she realize that those words could be taken more than one way? And the way that had flitted through his skull had better be discarded immediately. There was no starting over for them.

"Well, now you're back."

She nodded. "Now I am."

He turned left at the next stoplight. "We're almost there." The streetlights would start popping on soon. Tourists were always warned not to go out after dark, and maybe it was wise advice. But the best advice of all was to look like you belonged here and to not present any temptation.

Vivi definitely looked like she belonged. But temptation? She was that. But he was not about to admit that to anyone, not even himself.

He found a place to park in a public lot and paid the attendant. Then they walked the short distance to the funicular station.

"The *ascensor* is just ahead."

Unlike the ubiquitous street art that adorned many surfaces of the city, the funicular cars and stations had been painted in a linear pattern by professionals. At least the ones that were still in good repair. Cris paid for the tickets, shaking his head when Vivi started to pull out her wallet. "Next time."

Since there probably wouldn't be a next time, it was an easy way to be able to do something nice for her. Just like her offer to keep him company. He'd appreciated it more than she would ever know. He had a few friends, but most he kept at arm's length and he wasn't sure why. Maybe the niggling fear of loss that never quite went away? Maybe because he just didn't do much outside of parenting Gabi and work. Most friends did want you to at least spend some time with them. He used to go to sporting events, but that was before Lidia died.

Maybe he should start doing some of those things again. His aunt and uncle had offered time and again to watch Gabi, and Guilherme had invited him to go to various soccer events, but Cris had always found some excuse not to go. Instead, he'd stayed at home watching the game on TV.

They went through the turnstile and got their seats in the small car and waited for it to start up the hill. There were those who were dressed for dinner out, since Cerro Alegre had a lot of nice boutique-style hotels and restaurants. It was also a big hit with tourists, since it boasted a scenic overlook of the bay.

Then the funicular started moving. A slight sound next to him made him look at her. "Are you okay?"

"Yes, I'd just forgotten how steep a climb this is. I probably shouldn't look back."

He smiled. "That's why a few of these things are still in use. They don't take up the real estate that a road would need to navigate the hill. They can climb almost straight up. And it's not quite as scary as a ski lift would be, right?"

"I wouldn't know. I've never been up one of those and have no intention of doing it anytime soon."

"Your dad never took you to the Portillo ski resort?"

"No. He never did. He's never been a big fan of the cold, even though I would love to see snow."

An interesting fact that he'd never known about Vivi's dad. But that made sense. She'd grown up in south Florida, which boasted warm weather most of the year. "Santiago doesn't get very cold either, so almost no chance of seeing snow there. Or here, for that matter."

"Nope. Maybe someday, though. As long as it doesn't involve a ski lift."

The *ascensor* made it to the top and stopped with a loud squeak to let its passengers off. Fortunately, the way the funicular had been built kept the actual car level the whole ride up, so it didn't feel like a steep incline, even though it was.

They got off and went to the lookout. By now the lights had come on and although it wasn't pitch black yet, the view of the Valparaiso Bay was spectacular. There were some tall buildings, but they didn't obscure the view of the boats and the lights shining off the water. In the remaining daylight, the bay looked midnight blue, the deep color drawing you in.

"*Dios.* I'd forgotten. How I'd forgotten…"

Her words drifted away, but they carried a thousand sentiments that he recognized: familiarity, love…loss. Hadn't he thought that about his parents and wife? He could remember the second that he could no longer summon his mom's voice in his head. He'd tried for months, picturing her face and the movements of her mouth, but not the sound of her laughter, or the way she told him she loved him. It had been an awful time when he'd still been grieving Vivi's absence, and his parents were killed barely a year later.

"I know."

She turned to look at him. "You do, don't you."

"Yes." His eyes sought out hers. "And for what it's worth, I really am sorry about your engagement."

"He left me."

"Hell. I'm sorry, Viv." He knew all too well that loss was not always associated with death. In his mind, he'd always hoped that Vivi was as happy as he'd been during his marriage to Lidia. But it seemed maybe that wasn't the way things had gone for her.

He wasn't sure what else to say, so he stood there with her for several long moments looking out over the water. Then he felt the tentative touch of a hand over his, even though she never said a word. He turned his own palm up and curled his fingers around hers, never looking at her, but the familiarity was there all the same. He forced himself to just enjoy her presence and companionship in a way that he hadn't felt since…

Well, in way too long. And he didn't want to go there. He just wanted to stand here with her and not think about anything else. Maybe she felt the same way. Maybe she needed a few minutes not to think of the heartache of having a fiancé walk out on her.

Someone bumped against him as a person tried to squeeze in to take in the sights. It forced Cris to press shoulders with Vivi. He thought about moving away, but he didn't want to. He would have to go home sometime tonight and he wanted it to be with a good memory rather than the tragedy that had happened to Clara today. Even Roni had been weighing heavily on his mind. Both of their lives had changed in a split second.

And so had his. And evidently, so had Vivi's. Enough so that she'd left Santiago to come back to Valparaiso. And he couldn't help the feeling that came over him: he was glad she'd returned. Whatever the reasons.

On impulse, he let go of her hand and draped his arm around her shoulder. The only reaction was her burrowing closer. He closed his eyes and breathed in deep, the warm air filling his lungs with the scents of the water below and Vivi's own personal fragrance that was reminiscent of vanilla and citrus. Yes. He remembered. But only after capturing the scent for the first time in twenty years. Wisps of her hair blew in the breeze every once in a while, sliding across his cheek. That he remembered too. How those long strands felt against his face, against his arm, and sliding through his fingers as he kissed her long and hard.

He would have married her had she stayed. He knew that deep within his being. But if that had happened, he wouldn't have Gabi or have had Lidia and it was an exchange he was not willing to make, even if he'd known ahead of time the heartache that would await him later.

When another strand of her hair blew across his mouth, he lifted a hand to brush it away and ended up holding the silky soft section for a few brief seconds before setting it back in place. What kind of man would leave her? She hadn't said it outright, but he got the feeling that she'd been blindsided by the breakup.

He wasn't sure if it was an attempt to comfort her or for some other reason, but he slid his fingers in the hair by her nape and let it slide back through like a waterfall, something he'd habitually done when they'd been a couple. It had become muscle memory after thousands of times doing it. And he blamed that now.

But when he did it a second time, she turned toward him with a warm smile. There was something secretive behind her eyes, and he realized this was what he really wanted. For her to look at him like she had in the past. Just once. With a mixture of want and need that had almost driven him to do things that he knew their parents wouldn't approve of. But he didn't. And how he'd regretted that in the days after she'd left. He'd wished they had done it. Wished her wanting to have a baby with him. Anything that would have kept her there.

But then again. Where would they be if that had happened? Would Vivi have gone after her degree? Would he have gone to medical school knowing the grueling hours that it would bring?

And that meant Lidia and Gabi never would have been in his life.

No. He'd done the right thing.

But he was older now. Old enough to know that one thing did not necessarily lead to another. And that he didn't need or want anything that would bind her to him anymore. When her fingers reached up to touch his face, though, he knew he was lost. He wasn't sure if her thoughts were moving in the same direction as his were, but he wanted to experience what he had not back then. It didn't have to mean anything for either of them. And maybe it would even bring a closure that they'd never gotten. And maybe it would help whatever heartache Vivi was still experiencing from her breakup. He caught her hand so that she would look at him.

"Do you want to stay here and sightsee some more?"

She shook her head. "I want to go."

Taking a deep breath, he leaned down. "Where? Home? If no, then…?"

She went up on tiptoe, her lips touching his jaw and moving along it until she reached his ear. "Can you guess?"

He could guess a whole lot of things. But this was one thing he needed to be sure of.

"I think I need a little more to go on."

Her teeth nipped her ear. "That might get us kicked out of here."

Sensation traveled straight down the midline of his abdomen making a beeline for a place where, if noticed, might also get them kicked out of there. "I know a place."

"I don't care where."

The images those words drew up were insane. Of them naked in the bay below them, with him drawing her onto his hips. Of Vivi on the grass in some park, reaching up to pull him down to her. Of showers and beds and countertops, of bare tile floors. He would have rejected none of them.

Taking her hand, he towed her behind him as he left the lookout area and headed toward a hotel that he knew. One that he'd used a time or two in the past. But once he got there, he bypassed it for the one two doors down. One he'd never been to. With anyone. And he wasn't sure why it mattered. But it did. He wanted none of those other memories tainting the ones he was about to share with her.

They went in the door to the hotel, and he let go of her hand to go up to the reception desk.

CHAPTER SIX

VIVI HALF EXPECTED that she'd misunderstood him. That despite the intimate little touches, the talk about sightseeing and going home and wanting to know where else she wanted to go might have meant just that.

And yet here they were in the lobby of one of the fancy little hotels in the Cerro Alegre district and he was registering them as Mr. and Mrs. Diaz. Not even a phony name. Just a phony relationship. Because they weren't married and this wasn't about relationships or promises—it was about the here and now and needing something that only he could give. On the heels of hearing from Estevan again, she found that she needed it. Needed to know that she was still attractive. Still desirable.

He came back with a key card. "Third floor."

This was really happening. On the third floor. Somehow the thinking part of her brain filed that away in her memory banks to be retrieved later on.

"Elevator or stairs?"

His brows went up. "Is that a challenge?"

She blinked and then tilted her head up to look at him. "I think we might be arrested. I'm pretty sure they have cameras in both of those places."

He bent down and kissed her mouth, and that first touch of his lips against hers made her shudder as a thousand memories came over her. His arms went around her waist and drew her to him, as his head turned to deepen the kiss. She buried her fingers in his hair and pressed herself against him, taking in the sensation of his body against hers. And although they were both fully clothed, Vivi swore she'd never felt the intimacy that she did at this moment. With this man. And she had no idea why that was.

He finally lifted his head, dark eyes staring down at her. "The last thing I want is to be arrested. At least not yet."

She shivered when his meaning came across and leaned into him. *Dios!* This wasn't a dream. He really did mean to take her up to a room and share a bed with her. "Elevator, then. It's faster."

There was no wait and no one in the car when the doors opened. But when they boarded and the doors closed, she nodded at the corner where there was indeed a camera in plain sight. "See?"

"There won't be one in the room. There'll just be me…and you." He swept in to kiss her again, and suddenly she wasn't worried about cameras or the police as his tongue slid deep into her mouth. His hand at the back of her head, he held her there as he made his intentions very clear, turning her whole body red-hot. He could have taken her right then and there and she would have let him, consequences be damned.

But the elevator arrived at the third floor with a loud ding, which sent them—like fighters in a ring—back to their respective corners. Then he held his hand out and she took it, weaving her fingers through his as they disembarked with him glancing at the key card and then making his way down the hallway and a short string of doors. "Here. Three-oh-nine."

She squeezed his hand until he looked down at her. "Are you sure you're okay with this? I won't expect anything more from you than one night."

She'd said the words, but could she stick to them? One night and then it was over? If not, then it was going to be over before it even started, and she couldn't bear that thought.

"I won't expect anything more either, I promise. I just always wondered."

"Me too. You were always the one who wanted to wait."

He chuckled and handed her the card. "I know. I was a fool."

Vivi had no trouble swiping the card across the reader, hearing a satisfying click as the mechanism unlocked. She pushed the door open and went in, sensing him behind her.

The room was more spacious than she expected with white linens and pale beige walls. There were touches of color in blues and greens, probably meant to echo the water in the bay. She walked around, touching things, nervous all of a sudden. She could say it was because it had been a while since she'd been with anyone, but that would be a lie. She'd been with Estevan a little over a month ago. But this was different. The hum of anticipation was stronger than anything she'd felt with her ex.

Cris was right. It was because they'd both wondered what it would have been like for

them to have been together. And that anticipation was...

"What are you thinking?" His low voice
came from behind her and she turned toward
him.

"I'm thinking how much I want this."

His arm went around her waist and he
reeled her in. "Good. Because I was thinking the exact same thing."

Her palms splayed on his chest, relishing
the feel of him against her for the first time
in all those years. "I can't believe we never
did this. I wanted to, you know."

He smiled in a way that made her pulse
quicken. "I know. I wanted it too. I just didn't
want to..."

"Didn't want to what?"

"Rush anything. I wanted us to be sure.
And then time ran out."

"Yes, it did."

His hands cupped her face. "Until now."

Bending toward her he kissed her. Really
kissed her, as if they had all the time in the
world. And for tonight, they probably did.
And it was old...and new...all at the same
time. They melded together to form something that was unique to both of them. Her
arms wrapped around his neck trying to hold

on to him in case he might try to back away. But he didn't. If anything, he moved closer, crowding her and cocooning her all at the same time. It was decadent that she could be standing here with the man she'd once loved and be about to make love with him for the first time ever.

She wanted to rush and have him take her in an instant, and she also wanted it to go so slow that time stood still and became an eternity.

When his head finally came up, he looked into her eyes for a long time, and as if satisfied with what he saw there, he scooped her up in his arms and carried her to the bed in the middle of the room. "Do you have to be home tonight?"

"No." The word came out breathlessly, because it meant he wanted to take his time, too. The thought of having sex in various places in the room filled her with need and want and so many other things.

They'd done some heavy petting in their day. So heavy that, looking back, she'd been amazed at his control. And that control intrigued her now. How long could he hold out before going over the edge? How long could she hold on? Probably not as long as he could.

Dios.

He was still holding her, as if not quite sure what to do with her. Hopefully he wasn't having second thoughts. "Cris?"

His smile was slow and decadent. "Just going through my options."

"We have options?"

"Mmm…we do. Shower? Bed? Against the plate glass windows in the dark? In front of the bathroom mirror with me pleasuring you until you cry out—all the while watching yourself as you come apart?"

Her mouth went dry. Her list sounded so much tamer than his did. And she wanted his.

He turned from the bed and headed to the bathroom and suddenly she knew which one he was going to choose. For a second she thought she was going to explode right then, but somehow she kept it together long enough to get inside the room.

Cris didn't bother kicking the door shut, because there was no one there to see. No one there to hear anything. No one except for them.

He set her down in front of a huge mirror that spanned the space between two sinks and along a huge vanity. His arms went around her waist and he crowded her against the hard surface of the vanity. She could feel him in the small of her back, already hard, already ready.

He nuzzled her hair aside and kissed her neck, slowly working his way up until he was at her jawline. He pressed his cheek against hers and stopped there, meeting her eyes in the mirror. She sucked down a quick breath, when his hands slid up her belly and cupped her breasts, squeezing gently.

"So soft. So full. I can't wait to taste them." He found her nipples and rubbed his thumbs over them, sending a wave of heat straight down. "Do you *want* me to taste them?"

She tried to make her voice work, but whatever came out sounded strangled, so she had to nod instead.

His hands bunched her shirt, pulling it up so that his hands could tunnel under it. But he didn't stop there. He also slid under the band of her bra and then his skin was against hers. And still he held her gaze in the mirror. She could see herself bite down on her lip as the sensations grew more intense, then she shut her eyes only to have him sharpen the pressure until they flew open. "I want to see your eyes. Want to watch your pupils expand as you grow more and more aroused."

As if to highlight his point, one of his hands moved and dipped under the elastic waist of her cotton skirt. When they edged beneath the band of her lace undies, she shuddered, knowing what was coming. He was going to do exactly what he said he was going to do. Watch her while she watched herself have an orgasm under his touch.

"Cris…" She wasn't sure if it was a plea for mercy or for him to continue, and he didn't ask. And she didn't say no. Because he wasn't the only one who wanted this. She did too. Estevan had never done anything remotely like this. Had never rumbled words against her skin and then moved to carry them out.

His fingers moved further down, over her bare belly, over her mons until he reached the juncture between her thighs. At his first touch, her hips jerked forward.

"Yes, Vivi. I like that." His touch moved further, dipping over her. "You're so warm. So wet. I can't wait to feel you squeeze me to completion, can't wait to push so deep that I can't tell where you end and I begin."

He set up a slow rhythm of sliding across her, and she couldn't stop herself from joining him, moving her hips back and forth in time.

She rocked back and forth and then suddenly he stopped his own movements.

She blinked, looking into his face.

"Shh… Move, Viv. I want you to do it. I'm right here. Sharing in it. But I want you to use me for your own pleasure." He nudged her with his hips and she felt herself slide over the finger that was pressed against her most sensitive spot. "Just like that, *querida*."

His hips backed off and she couldn't take it anymore. She wanted it all, wanted to experience this through his eyes. So she did as he asked and moved against him and it was luscious. And when his finger curved and entered her, the world turned into vibrant colors that she didn't even recognize. She pumped her hips against him, feeling him slide into her and over her at the same time.

His other hand pulled her blouse and bra up over her breast, baring it, and then he gripped her nipple between his thumb and forefinger and squeezed it every time her hips moved forward. It was exquisite and moving and she couldn't help but feel her whole existence was about to undergo a huge shift.

Her movements increased as the need within her grew, and the whole time Cris was there, pressed close, the cradle of his arms supporting her, holding her, whispering to her, and she could tell he was as enraptured by what was happening as she was. She wanted to give them both what they wanted. *Dios,* and she wanted it now.

Now!

The tide rose within her, its current fast and strong, carrying her in its rush to reach its destination. Her hips jerked over and over and her head fell back against his shoulder as raw sensation erupted within her, blotting everything else out.

She was vaguely aware of him moving quickly behind her, catching her as her legs gave out. Then he picked her up and carried her to the bed and, peeling the coverlet back, set her gently down on the cool soft sheets.

Blinking up at him, she felt him climb in beside her and hold her, his arms nestling her against his side. She'd expected him to rush and enter her and seek out his own pleasure, but instead, he murmured to her and stroked her hair.

She looked at him. "But you…"

His smile said it all. But as if to make sure she understood, he whispered. "Don't worry. The night is still young. And I have several more ideas to try out."

And as if a few moments ago had never happened, she felt her body reacting to his words, slowly waking up again. He'd said that, but she'd had her doubts that they would go more than one round. Maybe that's why he'd done what he had. Maybe he'd gotten a different kind of pleasure from watching her break apart in front of him.

Although she couldn't imagine anything more fulfilling than what had just happened.

But it seemed that Cris was pretty sure he knew otherwise. And she was happy to let him try to prove it. All night long.

Cris's cell phone pinged once, then twice. In the distance he heard a second phone go off as well.

Still in a kind of exhausted, trancelike state, he fumbled to reach the nightstand. But it wasn't his room and the body pressed to his back wasn't his...wife.

He fell back onto his pillow. The night came back to him in a rush. Every single guilt-ridden moment. He was in a nameless hotel with Vivi. A ghost from his distant past. The one he said he was going to avoid. The one he said he was going to be able to work with without getting involved. The one he said Gabi was never going to get a chance to get attached to.

And he could still keep the last of those promises, even if he'd shot the first two to hell last night. Because he'd gotten involved the first time he'd touched her. And now he was going to have to figure out how to extricate himself without hurting her.

But would she be hurt? She hadn't asked for anything from him other than what had happened last night.

His phone pinged again. And so did hers. This time she stirred against his back and moved to get her mobile device.

Then she turned in his direction. "Cris, wake up. There's an emergency with Clara."

"Clara?" He reached for his own phone and quickly scanned the text. "*Maldicion!* She's spiking a fever and her wound is seeping. I've got to go."

"I got the same text. I think they're reassembling a team knowing we're going to have to go back in."

He sat up and threw the covers back. "I was so sure I got all of the fragments out."

"It was an open fracture. Who knows what contaminants were in there or how deeply they were pushed into the tissues. It's not your fault."

Clara might not be his fault. But this thing with Vivi? That was his fault, only he didn't have the luxury of trying to figure out how to get back out of it right now. Right now, they needed to get to the hospital. "I'll go."

"I'm coming with you. Besides, you drove us to the funicular station, remember?"

That's right—he had. So there was nothing left to do but get dressed and put this all behind him.

He turned toward her to tell her, only to have her shake her head. "No need. It's okay. We both went into this knowing what it was. And now we can move forward." She smiled. "No more wondering. Now we know. And it was pretty damned good."

She sounded like she was going to have no trouble moving forward. Just categorize the night and file it away, never to be bothered by it again.

He wasn't so sure he could do it quite as easily. Especially not after waking up and expecting to find life just the way he'd left it four years ago. And that carried its own guilt. Even though he hadn't consciously tried to swap her out for Lidia. And yet his subconscious? Was that what it had tried to do?

He could sort through all of those things at a later time. Right now they both had somewhere they had to be.

They pulled on their clothes in silence, with Vivi dressing in the bathroom while he put his clothes on in the main room. They'd both showered last night, but they didn't have a clean change of clothes, so they'd just have to make do with what they had. When she came back out, fully dressed, he asked, "Do you need me to take you home so you can change?"

"I'll do that at the hospital. I always keep a couple of sets of scrubs in my locker in case I need to change after a surgery."

Not that she'd done that many at Valpo Memorial. But she probably had done that at her old hospital and just carried the habit over to the new one.

They hurried to check out. It was only five in the morning and so the desk clerk looked a little worse for wear, probably being at the end of his shift, but he did his job with a smile. Then they were on their way, catching the funicular and riding it to the bottom of the hill.

The drive back to the hospital seemed to

take forever and Vivi was quiet. A little too quiet. "Is there anything I can do to help make this go back to the way it was?"

"Do you want it to? I say we each just process things in the way that's best for us and then go on with our lives. Nothing's changed. Not really. We had sex. Damned good sex. But that was yesterday and now we've moved to a different day. We can leave it in the past, just like we did twenty years ago."

And, yes, she did make it sound easy. A little too easy. He looked at her a little closer trying to see some chink in her armor and finding none. It was like she was immune to regret or guilt or any of the things he'd woken up to this morning. Or maybe it was because she was still hurting from the breakup of her engagement to worry about anything else right now.

Yet another reason for him to regret what had happened. She'd obviously been deeply hurt, and yet there he was, ready to jump into bed without giving the slightest thought to how she might feel.

Mierda!

They got to the hospital and went their separate ways to change and check in. Cris promised to let her know what the plan was as soon as he'd been to see Clara and had read her charts. But at the very least, they were going to need to go in to flush the wounds again, because if bacteria got lodged in the hardware he'd installed they were going to have a devil of a time eliminating all of it. Worst-case scenario was that they'd have to redo some, or all, of the surgery and replace all the screws and plates. Best-case scenario was that they flush everything with an antibiotic solution and then put her on strong intravenous meds that would hopefully get rid of anything they might miss.

He went to his office and changed his clothes yet again and then headed to Clara's room. He found her flushed and murmuring things that didn't make sense. Not good.

The chart showed she'd been given the antibiotics he prescribed and all had seemed well up until an hour ago when her temperature had suddenly risen to a hundred-and-three degrees. Peeling her dressings back, he could see that there was indeed some seeping, and a red angry line marked an area next to the sutures. He agreed with the doctor who'd taken a look at her. They were going to have to go back in and pray that she hadn't developed a staph infection. Those kinds of infections could steal limbs or even lives if not stopped in their earliest stages.

He knew Vivi was right and it wasn't that his surgery was faulty, but more likely a pathogen from the environment had entered the wound at the scene of the accident. A pathogen that the first round of antimicrobial flushing hadn't reached. But he was determined this next round would get anything and everything that was in there. They could still stop this in its tracks, but they did need to work fast. He went from her room to the nurses' station and placed orders for a surgical suite and team. He was gratified to see that the hospital had been on top of this right from the first sign of trouble. Vivi wasn't the only one who'd been called in. Several other members of the original team were here, including the anesthesiologist.

When he asked if Clara had been told about her mother, they'd replied that her family had told her and that she'd seemed to go downhill from there. While he knew she would need to know about her mom, he also knew that the shock could cause her immune system to tank and allow anything that was in there to go wild. Which could be part of what had happened. And evidently the dad was still in pretty bad condition.

"What time are we scheduled for?"

"We're just waiting for Viviani and Dalton."

He frowned. "Vivi is here, but I don't know about Dalton. Were you able to reach him?"

"He's on his way." The nurse glanced at her chart. "You say Viviani is here? I don't show her answering her text yet. I have an alternate who is already here."

Mierda. She hadn't, because it hadn't crossed either of their minds to act independently. As if they'd heard individually rather than being together when those texts had arrived. "I know she's here because I saw her down in the lobby. We spoke for a moment. Maybe she typed out a reply and didn't hit send."

And there was the first batch of lies, signed, sealed and delivered. And if Vivi gave a different response, then he was toast. And yet there was no time for him to find her and get their stories straight.

This nurse doesn't care, Cris. She's just putting pieces into place, not sitting there trying to work out why Vivi didn't respond to her text.

"Okay, then, that takes care of that problem.

Dalton is just a few minutes out and they're prepping Surgical Suite One even as we speak. Clara is already in pre-op, and there are a couple members of her family who are coming in. Permission has been granted to do whatever we deem necessary."

"Good. I'll go scrub in then. Here's what I'd like to see in there." He handed the head nurse the list of medications he'd need for the wound-flushing and there were orders for the antibiotics he wanted to use after surgery was done. "I'll also want to take a sample to be grown to see exactly what we're dealing with."

And he hoped to hell that it wasn't MRSA, a staph infection that was resistant to many antibiotics. But if it was, they needed to know which ones could be used to fight it. Thankfully they had quicker ways of "typing" the infection nowadays and the ability to figure out the best way to attack it.

Vivi came up on the floor just before he headed out and he heard the nurse say, "I guess he was right about seeing you in the lobby. I wasn't sure you'd gotten my text."

Her eyes darted to his for a second before agreeing with what had been said. "Sorry. I meant to reply, but was in such a hurry to get here that I must have forgotten. Anything I need to know before I go scrub in?"

The nurse said, "We're still waiting on one team member so we're about fifteen minutes out from the patient being brought in. Can you hold off on scrubbing in until we get everything in place?"

"Sure. Just shoot me a text. I promise to reply this time. Sorry again. Is the cafeteria open? I think I need a sip of coffee."

"If not, there's a coffee pot in the lobby that's refreshed every hour."

"Great. Anyone want anything?" Her glance encompassed both him and the charge nurse, who shook her head.

He replied that he didn't need anything either. Caffeine tended to wind him up a little too much. He preferred to be slow and methodical in the operating room.

Unlike last night at the hotel?

Better not to even think about that right now or it was going to shoot his concentration to hell. And Clara deserved to have a surgeon who was fully attuned to accomplishing what needed to be done. Every time he turned around, something seemed to be telling him that last night was a mistake.

Something else that he wasn't going to

think about right now. Not if he wanted to be at his best. Thank God he had actually gotten a couple of hours of sleep last night. Not that he hadn't wanted to go another round or two with Vivi.

And there it was again. He watched the woman in question get on the elevator, their eyes meeting for a split second before the doors closed.

How was he going to get her out of his system? That was what last night was supposed to have been about. And yet, it seemed like she was now embedded in there somewhere, just like Clara's infection, and it was up to him to figure out how to get it cleared out so that it didn't recur.

And that was the truth. Last night was not going to recur. Not if he had any say in the matter. Because if it did, he was going to have even bigger problems on his hands than spending a sex-filled night with a former flame. It would mean that his whole plan to keep Gabi and his love life in two different hemispheres might be in danger. And that was not something he was willing to let happen. So he would figure this out one way or the other. And he was going to do it soon.

CHAPTER SEVEN

She hadn't seen Cris since Clara's surgery yesterday morning. She'd gone home for a couple of hours' sleep and then come back for her afternoon shift, checking on the girl almost as soon as she'd arrived—while she was in a good deal of pain, the procedure and meds afterwards seemed to be doing their job. She hadn't seen Cris once.

And today seemed to be headed in the same direction. At least so far. She didn't know if he was even at work today or if he was just holed up in his office.

Avoiding her? Maybe.

They hadn't spoken about what happened in that hotel room, either, and that was troubling. She at least wanted to hear that they could continue working together. That's what they had said, right? That it wouldn't affect anything. And after they woke up to their phones pinging, she'd said as much.

We both went into this knowing what it was. And now we can move forward.

Except she wasn't doing the greatest job with that. She wasn't moving forward. She was doing nothing but thinking about the night they'd spent together. She'd been able to do her job in the operating room, but his voice had made her senses come alive as he'd asked her to hand him one surgical instrument after another. She hadn't fumbled or hesitated, but she'd had a hard time not picturing him moving over her as they'd continued making love. On the bed, this time. And it had been even better than the first time, even though she didn't know how that was possible.

She got back to the nurses' station after checking on the patients that were on their floor and Elena was there waving at her. "Dr. Diaz asked if you could go down to the hospital administrator's office for some reason."

Dios. He wouldn't have found a reason to get rid of her, would he? Her heart contracted in her chest. She would never have taken him for the kind of person who would do something like that, but how well did she actually know him now?

You know him. You saw the real Cris when he was hunched in that chair broken up about

Clara's mom being killed. You saw the real Cris when he saw to your pleasure first and then still saw to it that the next time was just as good for you. You saw the real Cris when his daughter ran up to him and he made it clear that there was no one more special to him than she was.

A few of her muscles relaxed. There's no way he would have tried to have her fired. So this was about something else. "Okay, I'll head down there now. Is he there?"

"I'm not sure where he was calling from. I do know he had a visit yesterday afternoon from that soccer player he did the surgery on."

Roni had gone to see him? Did that mean he was agreeing to help with the program she'd talked about? If so, why hadn't Cris contacted her and let her know that they had a meeting today?

She went down to the first floor, trying to remember where that office even was. It was unreal that she'd been here just under a week and so many things had happened since then. She found the office and knocked.

"Come in."

She peered inside the door and saw not only Cris and Marcos, the administrator, but also Roni. She swallowed, feeling a little left out.

They'd planned this meeting and she hadn't even been invited. Until just now.

Marcos stood and came around to shake her hand. "Have a seat. From what I hear, you're the brains behind this idea."

So again, why was she just hearing about this now? Roni grabbed her hand as she moved to a chair next to him and gave it a quick squeeze. She smiled and greeted him softly. But when she glanced at Cris, he was looking straight ahead, not even acknowledging her.

"Roni called my office yesterday afternoon and asked to come and speak to me about an idea you had had." He smiled. "I was going to try to schedule a meeting with all of you next week, but a spot opened up on my calendar and Roni is anxious to get this project underway. He's a pretty persuasive person."

She swallowed. That's what both he and Cris had said about her. So why was the surgeon giving her the cold shoulder now?

Marcos nodded at Roni. "Do you want to tell them?"

"Sure." He looked at her. "When Vivi came to me with the idea, I felt like it was just a pep talk. A way to get me to start doing my physical therapy. That lady down in PT should be a soccer coach, by the way—she doesn't let me get away without trying my best. But when Vivi came and talked to me about it again, I could see that she really meant it. That she was excited that the hospital might be able to use me to help hurt athletes. But I needed to check with my team."

He slid a folder off Marcos's desk and handed it to her. "I didn't want to talk to you about it until I knew for sure. This is what they came up with and I think it's a solid plan."

Cris still hadn't said a word. She had to know. "Have you already seen this?"

"I saw it yesterday afternoon. You were with patients at the time, so I was going to talk to you this morning, but—" he did manage a quick smile that made her heart quicken "—I think you'll like it."

She opened the folder and started reading, her eyes widening as what it said hit her. Her head jerked to look at Roni. "I never meant that you should put up the money for the program."

"I wanted to. Listen, I came up from nothing. And the idea that I can help not only injured athletes, but other kids who are like me is something bigger than just me. If I can use my money for that, then it will be all worth it."

Roni was donating two million dollars to start an athletic support center in the hospital that included group sessions on how to cope after a life-altering injury…or any injury, really. A career planner that had a list of resources to help athletes plan for the future once their career on the field was over. And it included something that Vivi had never even thought of. A coach who would run two sports camps a year for at-risk kids. One for soccer and one for basketball, which was also popular in Chile. Kids whose parents couldn't afford to send their kids to any kind of camp. It meant buying a small parcel of land somewhere in the city where a soccer field could be set up. The salaries for the part-time coaches and group leaders would be paid out of a portion of the money that would be put into a fund. Roni would head up the soccer camp and they would need to find a coach for the other team.

She glanced at him. "This is amazing. Thank you for being willing to do all of this."

"Don't thank me yet. My team had one caveat, because they are all about the brand and keeping it going. They want it to be called The

Ronaldo Saraia Sport and Support Center."
His lips twisted as if unsure how they would
take the news.

She smiled. "I think it's perfect."

"Good."

Marcos held up a hand. "I have one caveat
of my own. Roni has agreed to it, but I need
you and Cris to sign off on it as well. You
had the initial idea and I'd like you to still
be a sounding board for any changes to the
program and Cris will need to be involved
on the medical side of the program, okay-
ing any kind of training techniques to make
sure they're good for kids' growing bones and
muscles. So saying that, I'd like there to be a
picture of the three of you together that will
go out in a press release announcing the new
program. Vivi, I believe you said this will be
the first one of its kind in the city."

She nodded, seeing now why Cris had been
so quiet. He didn't want there to be a picture linking the two of them that would be
out there for the world to see. Well, it wasn't
like they were announcing their one-night li-
aison to the world. It was a sports program,
for heaven's sake. "As far as I could tell it is."

Roni broke in. "My team also checked on
that aspect, and we couldn't find anything

other than the normal support groups that weren't exclusive to athletes, so hopefully the concept will catch on. Athletes expend a huge amount of calories and their diets reflect this. But if they can't play, that will need to be altered, so having nutritional advice as well as career advice is going to be important."

Vivi felt like she was stuck in some surreal world where people were talking but she was unable to completely understand what they were saying. She glanced at Marcos again. "So you're agreeing to let this go forward?"

"Just like Roni has a team, the hospital does as well and I'll need to get board approval. But since the money and support have basically just been handed to us on a silver platter, we would be fools to turn this down. And I think Roni is right. This could help a lot of kids. And a lot of adults for that matter. And putting my administrator's cap on, it would be great publicity for the hospital itself."

Marcos glanced at Cris. "Once we get approval, can you figure out a time to get the three of you together for a photo op? Roni and his people are going to look at land and then the hospital will also need to approve the location and make sure the taxes and so forth are manageable. It's just a lot of red tape and working between teams. But I can definitely see it happening. So it may take a couple of weeks, or maybe even a month."

"I can do that."

"Good. Then if there's nothing else?" He stood. "Roni, thank you again for helping Valpo Memorial. I think this is going to be a great addition to our current services."

"I'm glad to be a part of something that will hopefully outlive me. Let me know when you're ready to move forward or if your team has any concerns."

Marcos came around and shook the man's hand. "I'll be in touch. Thank you again."

They all filed out of the office and Roni, now sporting a cane rather than a walker, waved it in the air. "I've been working, see?"

"Did your physical therapist okay that?" The words may have been stern, but Cris's smile was anything but. He liked the soccer player. It was there on his face and in the way he clapped the other man on the back.

Roni gave him a rueful grin. "Yes and no. But I'm being careful, I promise. I have some coaching to do. I'm in talks to maybe even coach a professional team. But don't worry— the sports camp will be a high priority and will need to be included on any contract I sign. Well, I'm off to my torture session. Catch you later."

With that he slowly made his way to the hallway that led to the physical therapy wing of the hospital.

This time, Cris actually looked at her. "Well, that went faster than I thought it would."

"Me too. Did you just hear about the meeting this morning?"

"I did or I would have tried to warn you ahead of time."

She had to ask. "Are we okay, then?"

There was silence for almost a minute. "Why do you ask?"

Okay, he'd just gone from smiling to tense in the space of a few heartbeats. "I think it's obvious."

"I'd rather not talk about this at the hospital."

It wasn't like there were a whole line of people going back and forth down the hallway. So what was he afraid of? "I'm not going to tell anyone, if that's what you're worried about."

"I am worried. The nurse couldn't figure out how I knew you were here this morning or why you hadn't responded to her text. I can picture there being a thousand more little things like that that will be hard to explain away."

She snorted. "Well, unless someone actually saw us check in or leave that…place, no one will be any the wiser."

"Maybe I am overreacting." He sighed. "By the way, my aunt told me that she did some research on apartments and has a little list of possibilities made, if you're still open to going to look at some."

"Wow!" Her eyes widened. "I know you mentioned it earlier, but didn't want to get my hopes up. I do, for sure. Living in a hotel room is getting a little old, even though it's more like a bed-and-breakfast with really nice owners. But it would be nice to have a place of my own. I appreciate her doing this."

"And that's part of it. My daughter may be with her when you all go to look, since it would have to happen during business hours, and I'll more than likely be here at the hospital. If you could not give her any encouragement, I would appreciate it."

"Encouragement? Do you mean your aunt or your daughter?"

"Either. Both. Aunt Pat remembers you from…before. I already told her not to think along those lines, that it wasn't happening, but she can be willful. And Gabi has been through a lot in her life. I'd rather her not get…attached."

"To anyone? I mean what about her teachers? Her peers?"

"I think she understands that those people are not permanent—that they're a year or two at the most."

Now she understood what he was saying. He didn't want his daughter getting attached to her, specifically. Because he sure as hell wasn't going to. She didn't know why that was a kick in the gut, but it was. Yes, they'd all but said there was no future to them, but to have him act like they couldn't even be friends. Or rather, maybe they could, but she just wasn't allowed to be a friend who came around the house and hung out with him and his daughter.

"Don't worry, I don't plan on stalking you to get to her. Or vice versa. Your secret rendezvous is safe with me. And your aunt is a grown woman. I'll let her choose her friends." She knew her words had come out in acid shades, but she couldn't help it. When someone hurt her, she tended to give back in kind. Not to strangers, but to those she cared about. And as much as she hated to admit it, she still cared about him and had hoped they could find a path to friendship. But it seemed that wasn't the case.

He moved a step closer. "Vivi, I didn't mean it like that. I don't want Gabi hurt. It's why I've never brought any dates home."

"And why we had to use a hotel room, even when your daughter was spending the night elsewhere. I get it."

Tilting up her chin, he looked her in the eye. "That's not fair, and you know it." He lowered his voice. "The hotel was the closest place, and I didn't feel like either of us wanted to wait to get to one of our residences."

She took a deep breath. He was right. That had been the reason. But she got the feeling he probably wouldn't have brought her into his home even if they'd been making out right in front of it. "You're right. I'm sorry. You just reminded me of my dad for a minute and how you accused him of saying you weren't good enough for me. I'm evidently not good enough for your daughter."

He sighed. "No, that's not it either. I just don't want her to assume we'll end up together. Relationships are too uncertain. You just broke it off with your fiancé, didn't you?"

"Yes." It was funny how he turned that

around to make it sound like she'd done the leaving and not Estevan, even when she'd told him it was her fiancé who'd made the choice. "So now that you've laid out the ground rules, I'll be sure to follow them. Although it might be better if I found another realtor. One who doesn't pose a danger to your comfort level."

He held up his hands. "I'm waving a white flag here. I don't want to fight. And I want you to use Pat. She wants to help. I just wanted all of us to tread carefully. And to keep Gabi off the playing field."

She smiled, knowing she'd overreacted, just like he'd mentioned doing moments earlier, and tried to move back to neutral ground. "I'll be on my best behavior, I promise, and try to make sure she stays on the bench. And I'm sorry if you thought I would do otherwise. I don't want to hurt Gabi any more than you want her hurt. So I won't encourage her. And if your aunt starts down that path, I'll head her off and assure her that neither of us wants a relationship. At least not with each other."

His sudden frown puzzled her. And she wasn't even sure he realized what his face was doing. Did he really think his aunt would try to play matchmaker? If so, she was in for a rude awakening, even if it didn't come from

Vivi. Her nephew had no intention of going back in time and renewing what they'd once had.

She was doing her best to hold true to that promise too. But when she'd thought her universe might be imploding in that hotel room, she was right. She just wasn't sure what the damage was and until she could mentally remove the rubble that had rained down on top of her, she would have no idea what was left unscathed. But there was this crouching fear that whatever remained was entirely different than what she'd hoped it would be.

He thought about that encounter long after she'd walked away, hips swishing as she made her way to her next destination. Cris knew that he had messed up royally in how he'd handled things today. But all during the meeting, he'd been hyperaware of the moment Vivi had entered the room. How she'd sat next to Roni. And how Roni had addressed almost all his remarks to her. She hadn't flirted with the man; in fact, he was pretty sure that she'd been unaware of his attention, but he could feel it in his bones. The man was attracted to her. He'd noticed it before, but today it seemed as clear as day.

It shouldn't matter. But somehow it did. He'd been irritated by it, like a clam with a grain of sand lodged in a sensitive spot. But when she'd stood in front of him a minute ago and said if they did wind up in relationships, it wouldn't be with each other, it had made him wonder if Roni wasn't the only one harboring a secret crush. If so, Vivi was a hell of a lot better at hiding that attraction than Roni was.

Imagining her coming apart for someone else the way she'd come apart for him was… unsettling.

And hell, it was a lot more than that. It was jealousy plain and simple, but it was also misplaced and unfair. He should want her to be happy. And he did.

So what was it, then? Did he just not want to know about it, the way his daughter would never know about their past relationship?

He wasn't sure. But then they'd come out of that room and he'd almost immediately thrown out that he didn't want her to try to be friends with Pat or with his daughter. How pompous and self-serving that had sounded. And she was right. He'd sounded just like her father, dictating who she could and couldn't fall in love with and who would go so far as to remove her from the vicinity if she dared trespass on forbidden ground.

And if Gabi started to like Vivi a little too much, would he do the same thing, swoop in and carry her away? He hoped he wouldn't. But at this point he couldn't promise. Because he might be in danger of liking Vivi a little too much himself. And he was doing his damnedest to backpedal and pretend that the night in the hotel hadn't happened at all. But it had and there was no going back. They'd slept together and that was going to hang between them for as long as they knew each other. He just hadn't thought through how to handle it yet.

But he'd better figure out a way that was a little more helpful and less like a warning gong.

Surely this didn't need to be as complicated as they made it out to be. Colleagues slept together from time to time and went on with their lives. What the hell was he so afraid of?

You're afraid you'll fall in love with her all over again, and that there's nothing you can do to stop that from happening.

Oh, yes, there was. He could be friendly and nothing more. Surely he could do that. And if he spent as little time as possible with her outside of the operating room where things were basically scripted and rehearsed until they ran like clockwork, that would be a first step. No more sightseeing tours. No more letting her comfort him, which she'd done after he'd operated on Clara.

And if she spent time with Pat and Gabi, what was the harm, really, as long as he didn't give them any reason to think that she might be a permanent fixture in their lives? There was none. At least that was his fervent hope.

Vivi was off on Wednesday, even though it was a surgical day. Actually she had asked for it off, citing that she still hadn't found a place to live. And that was true. She was planning on meeting Pat and going to look at a few places. But she'd also needed to decompress from everything that had happened over the last couple of days. She'd slept with him and then had almost immediately been whisked away to perform emergency surgery and then the next day she'd had the surprise meeting with Roni and the hospital administrator and then the confrontation with Cris afterward.

She needed time. In a place where she wasn't afraid of running into him or having to face him over an operating table. And she was looking forward to being outside the hospital and finding a more permanent place to stay.

She met Pat in front of the first of four apartments she would be looking at. When she arrived at the address, the realtor was already there. The woman exited the car and then went to the back seat to do something there. She realized quickly that it was to release Gabi from her car seat. Even though Cris had warned her that his daughter might be along for the ride, she felt a kind of nervous energy rise up inside her. She didn't want to say or do anything that might upset Gabi or Pat. But the second that the child's feet were on the ground, she ran over and embraced Vivi.

"Hi!" she said. "I remember you. You were with Daddy!"

Vivi couldn't stop the smile, despite the way the child had worded it. This was her second time seeing Gabi, but she was again struck by her uncanny resemblance to Cris. She even had a dimple on the exact same cheek as he did. Her heart lurched as a wave of affection crashed over her for the child. It was wholly unexpected and entirely...well, terrifying. She could see why Cris was worried. Gabi was absolutely adorable and anyone would be hard put not to love her at first sight. Like Vivi had done with the girl's father twenty years ago?

"Hi, Gabi. Your dad told me you might be coming along."

Mistake number one: she'd linked herself with Gabi's dad instead of just pretending to be a random client. She needed to be more careful. And she would be.

Pat came over and gave her a kiss on the cheek in true Chilean form. "It's so good to see you again."

"I know—it's been a long time." She embraced the woman.

Mistake number two: she'd assumed Pat was talking about the twenty years that had passed when she could have simply meant since their last meeting at the hospital.

She quickly added, "Thank you so much for helping me find an apartment. When Cris mentioned you were a realtor and probably wouldn't mind helping me with my search, I didn't expect you to drop everything. I hope I'm not putting you out."

"You're not—don't worry. This is what I do for a living. And I truly enjoy it. And the fact that it's for my only nephew makes it all the more special."

At first Vivi thought she meant that she was finding the apartment for her nephew, but then understood that she meant that she was doing him a favor. "Well, you have no idea how overwhelmed I was at the thought of finding something. My dad helped me find my place in Santiago, so I've never had to go out and scout properties before."

Pat motioned toward the apartment complex, and she had a key card that gave her access through the front gate. "Well, let's go look at the first one. It's a one-bedroom one-bath and on the second floor, but it's super-cute and the landlord is a dream. I know her personally." She gave a smile that was full of mischief, or at least that's what it looked like to Vivi.

"I can't wait to see it."

They went up the stairs. "The only downfall is that it's not on the ground floor."

"I kind of like going up stairs. It's like a built-in gym membership."

"Speaking of which, it's not far from where Cris goes to work out."

She swallowed, hoping that wasn't a hint. Especially since Vivi had seen the results of his workouts firsthand. And they were pretty incredible. She closed her eyes for a second to block out the images of the muscles in his arms rippling as he balanced his weight above her on the bed.

She didn't say anything, because she didn't think she could without her voice coming out as a squeak and giving her away.

There was a keypad on the front door. Once Pat punched in a number, a mechanism unlatched and the door swung open into a front foyer. There was a table with a beautiful silver bowl on it, obviously made to catch keys and small items as you came into the apartment. "Is it furnished?"

"It is. Although if you have your own furniture, the landlord can put this into storage."

"Really? They would do that? But no, I didn't save any of my furniture from Santiago, other than a rocking chair from my great-grandmother. My parents will have that sent once I find a place. So furnished is a plus."

She had the rest of her boxes in the room at the bed-and-breakfast. A couple of them had keepsakes that she hadn't had time to go through yet.

"The landlord has pretty good taste, if I do say so myself." There was again that smile, which was contagious.

"I agree. It's beautiful."

They went through an arched doorway and found a great room, a long table in the dining room acting to separate the kitchen from the living room. On one wall there were sliding glass doors that Pat went over to and opened to show a small balcony that was just big enough to hold a couple of chairs and a café table. It looked out over a pool area, which was empty at the moment.

It was quiet and peaceful, a few palm trees dotting the landscaping. "It's really a lovely complex. There's the pool, of course, and there's a communal party room where you can hold celebrations and so forth. It's equipped with a stove, fridge and a large serving bar. We've actually used it for a few of our own celebrations."

Wow, she must know the landlord really well for them to have allowed that.

The rooms were white stucco with beige furniture and green throw pillows. The same green fabric was on the seats of the dining room chairs. The contrast was beautiful as were the beams in the ceiling and the hardwood floors that Pat said went throughout the space.

Vivi loved it. It was exactly her taste. "Does it come with pots and pans and dishes?"

"Everything in here is included."

Unbelievable. The dining room table was made up with white china that was rimmed in gold, the simplicity of the place settings making it all the more elegant. There were olive green cloth napkins fanned onto each plate and a large wooden bowl in the middle looked like it was ready to receive whatever delicious food you chose to serve. She could see herself putting a large salad in there or meats that were cooked to perfection on the small grill she'd seen on the balcony.

"And we have the bedroom through here." Pat walked through the door, while Gabi stayed in the dining room and played with a couple of toys that the realtor had pulled out of her bag. The girl must be extraordinarily well-behaved to be left alone in there. But Pat evidently knew what she was doing.

The bedroom was just as gorgeous, the bed with a white damask coverlet that was turned down to expose white sheets that looked soft and welcoming. There was a green throw tossed across the lower third of the bed and an aged steamer trunk against the footboard.

There was also a long dresser that looked like it would hold every piece of clothing she owned.

"*Dios.* I never imagined… This is perfect."

Pat smiled. "You haven't seen the bathroom yet."

They went through the bedroom to the en-suite bath. Inside was a freestanding soaking tub with a beautiful chrome faucet set that had been placed at the side of the tub. It wouldn't interfere with the bather reclining their head on the sloped porcelain back. A live-edge board was placed so that it spanned the width of the tub, allowing the user to place a book or beverage and a candle on it to further enhance the experience.

The shower was small but certainly adequate, and chrome bars were mounted on the wall just outside the shower. They looked like they were heated. The place took her breath away.

"I'm afraid to ask how much this is."

Pat named a monthly amount, and Vivi's eyes widened. "Are you sure that's right? It must be worth twice that much."

"It's been sitting here empty for a while, just used to house family that fly into Valpo. The landlord is ready to lease it out, but will be very picky about who she leases to. It was hers before she was married and it was leased to other family members for years. It holds sentimental value. The whole complex was remodeled just a few years ago, which is why it's so nice."

"Will she even lease to a single woman?"

"She would lease it to you." Pat's voice was soft. "I can guarantee that."

"How do you know?" Vivi looked at her as understanding dawned. "You're the landlord, aren't you?"

"I am. Cris rented this place for years after he graduated from medical school before he and Lidia got married. Then they moved to a different place and got pregnant with Gabi."

That gave her pause. "What would he think about me living here?" To have an ex-girl-friend living in the apartment might not go over too well.

"It's mine to rent to whomever I please."

"I know, but…"

She touched Vivi's arm. "He won't care. He hasn't asked about this place since Lidia died."

"What happened to her?"

It was *so* none of her business, but the words came out before she could stop them. She knew how his parents died, but not how his wife had.

"She died of ovarian cancer. It was diagnosed almost as soon as Gabi was born. She died a year later. We were all devastated."

That was why she could leave Gabi playing in the other room while they checked out the rest of the apartment. "I think you should ask him before you agree to rent it to me."

"I promise, he won't care. He's happy where he is."

"Is this the furniture that was in here when he lived here?" She didn't think she could live there if it was. It seemed too personal, somehow. Especially if he and Lidia had made love in that bed after they started dating.

"No. I furnished it with new stuff after Cris moved out. I would just ask that we be allowed to use the party room for Gabi's birthday parties if Cris wants to hold them here."

"Of course. But your rent is way too low."

"No. It's the perfect price for the perfect person."

She tried again. "I can give you references."

Pat smiled, even as Gabi came into the room carrying the small doll her aunt had given her and leaned against Vivi's leg.

"I don't need them," she said. "My mind is made up, if yours is. But don't take it just because it's mine."

"I wouldn't. But I love it. Truly. And it's

a great distance from the hospital. I could jog in or ride a bike if I chose to. Would you mind my bringing my rocking chair in? I think it would look wonderful in the corner of the bedroom. And it would make it feel like home. My home. That chair goes everywhere I go. Do you want a year's lease?"

"How about we just go month by month. No deposit needed, and you can move in whenever you're ready."

She laughed. "How about this Saturday? I'm off duty and all I'd be bringing over would be my suitcases and some boxes of books and memorabilia. My parents could bring the rest when they come."

"Speaking of parents. The sofa pulls out into a bed and the curtains that are at the balcony are extralong and actually pull along a track you'll see on the ceiling and provide privacy for anyone sleeping on that couch. No need for them to find a hotel."

"I don't know how to thank you. I really don't."

Pat gave her a tight hug. "No thanks needed. It's so good to have you back in Valpo."

Vivi smiled. She'd been questioning her decision to come back ever since she found herself across the operating table from Cris.

Their time at the hotel had only added to her confusion and made her second-guess everything. But she couldn't go back to Santiago. It was a huge city, but not big enough for both her and Estevan. Even the thought of moving back there and possibly running into him made her queasy. The same feeling she'd gotten when she saw his text. She'd replied and asked him not to contact her again. So far he hadn't.

"Thanks. I'm hoping I made the right decision to come back."

Pat put her arm around her and leaned her head against Vivi's shoulder. "I think you are just what this city needed."

What a strange thing to say. Then she remembered Cris's warning not to encourage his aunt. Was this what he meant? Surely she wasn't talking about her nephew. Their relationship ended twenty years ago.

And that time in the Cerro Alegre hotel room?

That wasn't a relationship. It was a ticking time bomb. One that could very well blow up in her face. As could her decision to rent this apartment from Cris's aunt. But that's what she was going to do. Both because she loved the apartment and because it was the right price and in the right place. Just because it didn't come with Mr. Right didn't mean anything.

Dios. Cris was not Mr. Right. At least not hers. Her throat contracted when Gabi caught her hand and held on tight. But this wasn't her family. It was Lidia's and she was pretty sure Cris was not anywhere near moving on after her death or he would have done so by now. And he'd talked about protecting his daughter from being hurt. Who could argue with him about that? Certainly not her.

So did she shake her hand free of the child's grasp? No. Because that would be cruel and Vivi wasn't about to be that person. So she smiled down at the girl and hoped to hell she was doing the right thing.

And because he was bound to find out about her renting this place, she decided to take the bull by the horns and tell him the next time she saw him at work. Where she would assure him that she'd done nothing to encourage his daughter to like her. No matter how much she'd been tempted to do exactly that.

As they went back down the walk, Gabi was talking about a picnic with her dad that was set to take place today at a local park.

"You can come, Vivi. I'm sure Daddy would like it. You smell nice."

Her face flamed and she tried to discreetly take her hand back from the child's grasp, but Gabi's grip tightened.

"Oh, yes, you must. Guilherme and I will be there as well. I'm sure Cris won't mind. I'll call and ask him myself right now."

"Oh… I don't think that's a good…"

But Pat was already dialing. "Cris, hi! I'm not interrupting, am I?"

He was going to go through the roof. Vivi tried to wave and shake her head no, but Pat tilted her head like she didn't understand. "Oh, yes, she found the perfect place. At least she said it was." The woman sent her a smile that was so genuine that all Vivi could do was hunch there in misery.

"Yep, Gabi's right here with us. She asked Vivi to come with us on the picnic and I assured her it would be all right with you. It will be, won't it?"

She waited for Pat's face to change when faced with whatever Cris was saying at the other end of the line. But it didn't. She just smiled and then gave Vivi a thumbs-up sign. He'd said yes? That was almost unbelievable.

And it only made her stomach shrivel up even further than it already had.

"Okay, we'll see you in a couple of hours, then. Love you."

Then she disconnected the call and acted like all was right with the world. Little did she know that she'd just helped Vivi to commit mistake number three. And that was to accept an invitation to lunch issued by his daughter. She honestly believed Pat was trying to be friendly and that there'd been nothing nefarious about the invitation. But it still didn't make her feel any better. She just hoped that Cris knew that she'd had nothing to do with being wrangled into a family gathering. If not, then she hoped she could convince him of her innocence.

CHAPTER EIGHT

CRIS DROVE TO the park amused, rather than irritated. His aunt and his daughter were both strong-willed when they wanted something. And it was partially his fault that Gabi had been with Pat this morning when she'd taken Vivi apartment hunting. Evidently, they'd found "the perfect one." Which was great. Because now he could show up at the park and pretty much be assured that it would be the last time that his daughter would have an outing with the scrub nurse.

So if he could make it past today, it should be smooth sailing from here.

He parked in the lot and got out of the car and stretched. Soon Gabi came sprinting from a nearby picnic area and grabbed his hand. "Bivi is here too!"

His nose wrinkled. "You mean Vivi."

"That's what I said. Bivi."

The woman in question was over at the

table helping his aunt set up the food and his mouth went dry. She was wearing the same gauze skirt and blouse that she'd been wearing the night they made love. There was no way she'd done it on purpose, since she hadn't even known about the picnic until this morning.

And she wasn't meeting his gaze. Probably because she was horrified at being roped into this monthly picnic thing. It normally happened on Saturdays, but Pat had something with a group of friends this week, she'd said.

Gabi pulled him toward the group. His uncle was already at the grill, and the smell of steaks filled the air, reminding him that he hadn't eaten since breakfast. He'd had back-to-back surgeries this morning and then a meeting that he'd just come out of.

"Cris! I was wondering if you were going to make it. We were getting worried."

He glanced at Vivi, but she still wouldn't meet his eyes. After the lecture he'd given her on not letting Gabi get too close, who knew what she was thinking. The best thing they could do was get through this in one piece. But first he had to reassure her that it was okay.

He decided to make the first move. "Glad you could make it, Vivi."

Her head swiveled toward him and a look of utter shock came over her. This was evidently not the reaction she'd expected out of him. And he could see why. Maybe it was time for him to lighten up. For all Gabi knew, Vivi was simply a friend and a genuinely nice person. Why would she think otherwise? It wasn't like Vivi was stepping into any kind of substitute mother role. And he believed her when she'd said she wouldn't purposely lead Gabi on. It was what had helped him keep his cool when his aunt had sprung the news on him.

He'd had time to think things through after he'd gotten off the phone with her.

"Thanks. I couldn't turn down the invitation."

She gave him a pointed look that said, *Really, I couldn't turn it down. They wouldn't let me.*

"I know." The words were accompanied by a nod that he hoped conveyed his understanding.

She blew out an audible breath that made him laugh and pull her aside. "That bad, huh?"

"I expected the phone to explode in her hand when she called you."

"It's okay. We'll just go with the flow and in a couple of hours it'll be all over."

Pat interrupted them. "I think we're ready, if you're hungry."

"Famished," Cris said. And he realized it was true. He was hungrier than he could remember being. And he actually was glad that Vivi was here.

Because that meant she wasn't out with Roni?

Not fair, Cris. Just get over it.

But as they ate and he watched Vivi laugh at the terrible jokes that his uncle told and let Gabi talk her into letting her sit on her lap, Cris got a warm feeling in his chest that he recognized from four years ago. He and Lidia used to attend these family picnics and it felt very much like this. But instead of the loss and crushing grief that he'd felt at these events since her death, today he was able to look back at those times with an affection that had become almost foreign.

He quickly shook the feelings away. But what he couldn't shake away was the fact that he was able to enjoy watching Gabi hang out with a woman who wasn't his aunt. Not that anyone had ever attended these picnics with them before.

It wasn't the disaster he'd envisioned it being. And when it was time for Vivi to go, citing that she needed to do some things before heading back to her hotel, Gabi didn't pitch a fit or cry or do any of the things that he'd been afraid she would do.

Maybe it was going to be okay. Gabi had made a friend, and it had happened seamlessly and without trauma.

As they waved goodbye to her, he hugged his daughter tight, both proud and afraid of how much she'd grown over the past year. One day she would be an adult and on her own. And then he would be free to pursue his own dreams. Except Cris wasn't sure he had any of those anymore. And if he did, his heart sure wasn't sharing those dreams with his mind. And maybe it was better that way.

Come dressed for a picture.

She hadn't checked her hospital email in a day or two and when she opened it up this morning, she saw this caption on a message from Marcos. *Dios!* She checked the date. It was for today!

She'd just finished moving into the apartment over the weekend and still hadn't told

Cris about renting it. She just hadn't found the right time, since it had been crazy at work. And at the picnic, he'd been in such a good mood that she'd been afraid of somehow destroying that.

And that picnic had been so much fun. Almost too fun. She kept waiting for the other shoe to drop, but it never had. Unless there was some kind of delayed reaction.

She'd had two surgeries on Wednesday and Thursday with Cris. But they'd barely spoken other than him asking for surgical instruments. She wasn't sure if that was on purpose or if he was simply stretched for time. He didn't come into the room until just before the surgery started and didn't stick around after it ended.

And she hadn't heard any more from Roni about the new project either. Until now. And it seemed like she was going to have to pose for publicity pictures with both Roni and Cris. And she immediately felt sick. All she could hope was that the pictures were individual ones and not ones where they would have to pose together. She wasn't even sure why she was so fearful of having them done. The picnic had been good and fun.

If anything, maybe it had gone too well.

Maybe Cris's quietness in the operating room was a delayed regret about letting her spend time with his daughter. Although she hoped not.

The other thing that made her queasy was that she had opened a small box of keepsakes, expecting to give it a quick perusal and tuck everything back away. But out had tumbled a small ring with familiar red crystals.

The ring Cris had given her twenty years ago. She didn't even remember keeping it. She'd stared at the thing for close to fifteen minutes, trying to will herself to toss it back into the box and tape it shut. But she couldn't make herself and she didn't know why. So she'd set it on the dining room table until she could figure out what to do with it.

And now she had to pose for pictures with him. She wasn't sure she could do it.

She'd been instructed to wear clothing in light colors. She didn't have much that fit that description except for that gauze skirt she'd worn for both the trip to Cerro Alegre and to the picnic. But if she paired it with a pale pink top, Cris wouldn't recognize it as such, would he?

Dios, she hoped not.

She took care in getting ready, brushing her

hair until it shone and then pulling it up in a high ponytail. It was a look she deemed cool and professional. No sexiness to it. And that's what she wanted. The last thing she wanted was for Cris to think she was dressing for him in hopes of getting another night with him.

Not that she would turn him down. Once she'd gotten used to the fact that she hadn't committed professional suicide by sleeping with a coworker, she'd started to relax a little. Especially after his laid-back attitude at the picnic. It had been a week since their night together and the world had kept on turning. She'd spent a few more hours in the company of both his aunt and his daughter as they signed forms required by the condo association and switched the electricity and gas from Pat and her husband's names into hers. And although Gabi had taken to hugging her tight, she hadn't started to call Vivi mama—which she was pretty sure was one of Cris's biggest fears. Instead she called her Bivi, which warmed her heart in a way that made her uneasy.

She could admit that she was smitten with his daughter. She was charming and smart and well-adjusted. She talked nonstop about her preschool and all the friends she had there. Vivi loved listening to every word the girl uttered. But Cris was never going to know about any of that, because she was not going to tell him. And she was pretty sure that Pat wouldn't either. His aunt seemed oblivious to it. Or maybe she just wasn't worried. But if she'd seen Cris's face when he'd warned her not to encourage his daughter, she might be.

Looking at her reflection and blowing out a breath, she deemed herself as ready as she'd ever be. She glanced at the ring on the table with a growing sense of foreboding before locking the front door. On a hanger she carried a set of scrubs with her to the car so that she could change into them as soon as the pictures were done. Hopefully it wouldn't take long. And then afterwards she could tell him that she'd moved into the apartment he used to occupy.

She would much rather the news come from her than from Pat. And she would just act surprised if he said he'd once lived there. She hadn't died from anything that had happened so far. So this would just be one more hurdle to get over before the road cleared and they could go on as if nothing had happened.

At least she hoped that was possible and

that he wasn't avoiding her for some unknown reason.

Clara had been released, her infection almost totally cleared, although her father was still in a coma and it had been touch and go for the past week. There was no word on how the girl was dealing with her loss. All Vivi knew was that she was staying with close relatives until her father got better. Vivi prayed for that to happen with all that was in her, even lighting a candle for the man at the church she had attended with her family.

The drive to the hospital took less than fifteen minutes, despite the traffic this time of morning. She could almost run it in the same amount of time, but since she didn't want to arrive at the hospital hot and sweaty or try running in her wedged heels, she opted to drive.

Parking in the employee lot, she picked up her purse and the hanger containing her scrubs and walked through the front doors to the hospital, then stopped dead. The foyer had been transformed into a soccer field, complete with two goals and what looked like artificial turf where the information desk had once stood. And there was photography equipment set up along one wall. On the other side was a set of barricades that formed a narrow corridor where hospital visitors could come and go without interfering with the setup.

But it looked like people were standing along the barricades, hoping to catch sight of Roni, whose picture covered almost one entire wall where a vaulted ceiling allowed it to stretch upward to around twenty feet.

She'd hoped these pictures would be done in the conference room or something, which was where pictures for staff lanyards were taken. It looked like the press release, though, was going to be a public event.

Had the email said anything about this? She couldn't remember. And right now she was stuck in that corridor with all the other gawkers and feeling more and more self-conscious by the second. Especially dressed as she was. Hopefully no one would guess who—

"Vivi, there you are. Come on through." Marcos stood holding a gate open so that she could step onto the Astroturf. There was a crunchy feel as she walked over the surface and she could almost feel the whispers of the onlookers as they tried to figure out who she might be.

Well, she could tell them. She was just a nobody and wasn't sure exactly why they needed her picture. Or why they needed her on their brochure at all.

Marcos ushered her into a room on the other side of the foyer. They'd actually needed to cut the door out of the huge picture of Roni. And inside the room was the man himself, along with Cris and about ten people she didn't know. Maybe they were part of Roni's entourage or photographers or something. But all of a sudden this thing seemed blown so far out of proportion that she wondered if it had been such a good idea at all. She hadn't wanted the sports program to become a farce that was about any one person and she hoped Roni didn't want that either.

As if guessing her discomfort, Cris came over to her and whispered, "It's not as bad as it looks."

"Really? Because it looks pretty horrible from where I'm standing."

Roni came over to join them, still using his cane, enveloping her in a big hug before stepping back to give her a rueful grin. "Sorry for my big *rostro* messing up your hospital. But I've been assured that it will bring in even more money for the program. It won't be all about me. I promise."

She believed that's what he wanted and

what he thought. But right now it was going to be a hard sell as far as she was concerned.

He made his way back to where a big stack of books sat and then Marcos headed their way. "The photo op is going to be in about thirty minutes and will be open to the public by invitation only and with a donation. And Roni will autograph his biography and all of those proceeds will also go for the program."

"Why do you need us here at all? I'd rather this be about the program rather than about me or anyone else."

"It will be. But it has to get off the ground if it's going to work. Think about how new departments in the hospital get started. There's usually a group picture of the staff, along with a short bio of each member highlighting his or her contributions to the program."

She couldn't argue with him there. She'd seen the one that had been made up for the orthopedics team. She wasn't on it yet, but most of the other staff members were, as well as all of the physicians and surgeons. And she agreed. That's what drew people in.

Okay. She was willing to give them the benefit of the doubt. And for sure Roni was a huge draw, and she'd sensed during their initial talk that his heart was in the right place, so maybe she should trust what the experts said and just roll with things. Everything would probably pan out in the end.

Thirty minutes later, they were ushered out onto the fake field, where Roni held a soccer ball. She and Cris were placed a few feet back on either side of him. The rest of the PT staff were lined up behind all of them. So the effect was that of a large team of staff and at the center of it all was the biggest star of them all, Ronaldo Saraia. They took several pictures of the whole group, then the PT team were dismissed to go back to their department.

The hardest picture was the one they took of her and Cris together. They were asked to stand with their arms crossed over their chest and angled in to kind of face each other, although they were still looking forward at the camera. It was supposed to give them a look of authority while still working together as a team.

But all she could see was Cris as a person and not as a surgeon. And when they edged them closer together until their shoulders were touching, it felt very intimate and very public. Kind of like that voyeur scenario that he'd hinted at in the hotel about making love in front of the plateglass window. That one had never happened, and she wasn't sure she could have gone through with it if he'd wanted to unless she was sure they couldn't be seen.

But in this instance, she didn't have a choice. They were basically being asked to make love to the camera with an actual audience standing there watching. It was surreal and she felt very, very vulnerable about the whole thing.

When they were told their part was done, Cris squeezed her hand for a brief second as if realizing exactly how she was feeling, and she appreciated it more than he could imagine. She was glad it was over. And if they were asked to repeat any of the shots, she wasn't entirely sure she would agree. But Roni was now seated at a table in front of his picture on the fake field autographing books and a few soccer balls and other items that would be raffled at the end of the gathering.

Right now it all felt as fake as that field. She could only hope it ended up being worth the effort. Big promises came with even bigger expectations. Could she, Cris, Roni and the hospital deliver on them? She wasn't sure at this point. Maybe once they found the land for the field and were able to bring in some specialized staff for the counseling programs they'd talked about, it would seem more real—more feasible.

Marcos came over and shook their hands. "I just saw the digital proofs. They look good. We'll make sure you each get some copies of them."

The idea of having a picture of her and Cris together made her heart ache. She knew it was just about their professional union, but her heart said that it went beyond that. And the picture would just be a reminder of what had happened between them. Both twenty years ago as well as a week ago.

You don't have to keep it or display it in your home, Viv.

She knew that, but she was so afraid of what she might see reflected on her face in those pictures.

Because somewhere between the flash of lights and the clicking of camera shutters she realized something. Something that she'd foreseen happening as they'd made love that night. Her world had indeed imploded. And she'd done the unthinkable. She'd fallen in love with Cris all over again.

And it was both a thrill and a tragedy. Because he'd made it more than clear that he did not want a relationship. Not with her. Not with anyone. Because of his daughter. And very probably because of his late wife. He'd found love again after their childhood romance. And from what it sounded like, nothing was ever going to match up to what they'd had. She was glad he'd found that kind of love. But there was a little part of her that was jealous that he'd gotten the happy ending and she had not.

Happy ending? His wife had died. How was that happy?

It was happy in that Cris would probably do it all over again, even knowing what was going to happen. Maybe it would have been the same if she and Estevan had married. But she wasn't so sure. Their relationship must have had holes in the fabric that she hadn't seen. And when the wrong person had come along, it had all unraveled until there was nothing left.

Was that what that night with Cris had been about? Proving that she was still attractive as a woman? A rebound romance? If so, that plan had backfired terribly. But the biggest question of all was a crucial one: would she undo that night with Cris if she could? If it meant not realizing she loved him?

No. She wouldn't. Because she'd experienced something she thought was long beyond her reach. Something she never would have guessed possible. And she would cherish that memory for the rest of her life.

Cris gave her a quick wave and then left the area, probably headed to his own office. He hadn't sounded any more overjoyed than she had been at the offer of a free set of pictures of the two of them along with the shots with Roni and the other PT staff. For her own part, she would gladly display the one of the whole team. But the one of just the two of them? She didn't think so. Someday her children would probably find it tucked into a book along with that promise ring and ask who that man was.

She would simply say it was someone she'd once cared about very much.

Really, though? Did she think she'd have children? She was thirty-seven years old and her fiancé had basically run off with another woman. She didn't see herself starting over anytime soon. And since she was an only child, there would be no nieces or nephews. And her parents would have no grandchildren. Unless she decided to go it on her own. But then she'd probably need to move back to Santiago to have a support system.

It was no use, though, rushing into life-altering decisions. And, right now, railing against a loss she'd never experienced would solve nothing. So all she could do now was live her life and do good to others.

And that should be enough for her. And if it wasn't, then she somehow needed to make it enough. Because it was all that she had.

Gabi burst through the door to his office and leaped into his arms, making him laugh. He'd half expected Vivi to march in complaining about the pictures that had just hit his inbox. There were a couple that were real doozies. Because one of the group ones must have been taken before she realized what was happening and she was looking at him with this soft expression that made his heart lurch.

He forced his attention to move back to his daughter. "Have you never heard of knocking, Gabs?" He must have sounded more severe than he realized because her lower lip stuck out.

Pat came in, apologetic. "Sorry, Cris, she had some exciting news and wanted to tell you about it."

Now he felt doubly bad. He was letting his thoughts take over when he should be focused on the here and now. The things he *could* change and not the things he wished he could change.

"Sorry, *querida*. What's your news?"

"Ti-Tia is getting a new puppy and is going to let me choose a name for her. She's so cute! I picked her out and she loves me already."

His aunt and uncle had lost a dog a little over six months ago and had been talking about adopting one from an animal welfare agency.

"Well, Gabi," her aunt corrected. "She's not a puppy. Not really. But she does need a name."

Cris hugged his daughter. "That is exciting news. Is there a picture of this pup?" Because of their schedules, he and Lidia had never gotten a pet, so his aunt and uncle's dog had become kind of a communal pet, and he was grateful to them for letting her take a big part in its life.

Gabi jumped out of his arms and went over to Pat. "Can you show him?"

"Of course, honey." His aunt pulled out her phone and opened the camera. "She's going to be spayed and get her shots today and we should be able to bring her home tomorrow." She pulled up a couple of pictures of what looked to be a smallish dog that was definitely a mixture of breeds and that mix hadn't been the kindest, from the looks of her: pug nose, wiry hair and legs that looked far too long for her short body.

He looked up at Pat. "You didn't let her pressure you into this one, did you?"

His aunt chuckled. "She might not look like much, but she took a definite interest in Gabi and sat with her quietly as if sensing she needed to be gentle. And when we had to leave the enclosure, she gave the most pitiful howl and...well, I couldn't resist. I think she's going to make a great companion. Guilherme agrees with me. He was as taken with her as Gabi was."

"So do you have a name picked out?" he asked his daughter.

"Mollete. But I'm going to call her Molly for short."

He wasn't exactly sure the dog looked like a muffin, but kids saw things differently than adults did, he'd found. "I like it."

"She already knows her name. She's supersmart." His daughter was so sure of this that she'd popped her palms up, elbows tucked into her sides as if she had discovered a surprising fact.

"I'm sure you'll teach her lots of things. Like manners." He smiled.

Pat laughed. "To change the subject...did Vivi tell you that she's renting our old apartment?"

"What apartment?"

"The one that your uncle and I've had for ages. Don't tell me you don't remember it."

He frowned and then tilted his head. "The one I lived in during medical school?"

"Yep."

When he could speak, the words came out slowly as if he'd had to drag them out kicking and screaming. "I didn't realize you were going to show her that one."

"She's the perfect tenant. You know I wouldn't trust that apartment to just anyone. We did quite a few updates to it."

"Yes, I know." He'd once thought that he and Lidia would share that apartment. But she'd wanted something that was theirs and theirs alone and so he'd moved out and they'd found the place where he currently lived.

He hadn't been to that apartment in ages, except to have a couple of Gabi's birthday parties in the communal room in the complex. "When does she move in?"

Why had he asked that, unless he was actually toying with the idea of talking her out of it?

"She already did. Over the weekend."

"That was fast. Was there a reason for it?"

Pat shrugged. "It was my suggestion. She doesn't have any furniture to speak of and so it was only a matter of moving her suitcases and a couple of boxes over there." This time it was Pat who frowned. "Is there a problem?"

He realized he was making a bigger deal than necessary over a piece of property that didn't even belong to him. But it just seemed weird to think of Vivi as living in a space he'd once inhabited. But if he knew Pat, she'd downplayed all of that and maybe even strong-armed Vivi into taking the place. And she was right. Vivi would be the perfect tenant if her work in the operating room were anything to go by. She was meticulously careful and ultra-organized. It was as if she'd mentally catalogued all the instruments and their position on the trays in front of her. Except for that first surgery, she hadn't made a misstep yet. And even that one time it had only been a slight hesitation. He could understand why now. Because he'd been just as shocked once he realized his new scrub nurse was none other than his high school flame.

"No, it's not a problem. Just with our past, I'm surprised she would want to—"

"The only thing she was worried about was how you might handle her living there. I'm guessing she was right?"

It looked like she was. He was being a first-class *culo*.

"Let's just say your nephew is being a jerk. Of course it's okay that she lives there. It's a great space and I know she'll love it."

"She loved it the moment she set eyes on it. So please don't be a—how did you put it?—a jerk if the subject ever comes up."

"I won't. And thanks for telling me. It just caught me by surprise. I'm sure she appreciated the help in finding a place."

Pat came over and leaned down and hugged him. "It'll be okay, Cris. I just have a feeling deep down in my bones."

All his senses went on high alert again. "You would not be trying to do anything sneaky, would you?"

She stood up and glared at him. "I would not play around with your future. So no. If you're worried about me matchmaking, that never even entered my mind. Because if it had, I would be a lot better at it than that."

Which was exactly what he was afraid of.

But he no longer thought she had any ulterior motives in leasing the apartment to Vivi. And maybe he needed to make sure that Vivi knew he really didn't mind.

Even if it wasn't entirely the truth.

The buzzer rang at her front door just as she'd finished making her dinner of *chile relleno* soup, one of her favorite easy dishes. Pat had said she might stop by one of these days to check in on her, so thinking that must be who it was, she unlatched the door and opened it, eyes widening when she saw who it was.

It wasn't Pat. It was Cris, and he was standing there in all of his brooding male glory, hands stuffed in the pockets of his chinos, the sleeves of his blue dress shirt pushed up his forearms. The breeze outside lifted his hair off his forehead and sifted through the curls.

"Cris. What are you doing here? How did you even know I *was* here?"

"Pat said you were renting the place and mentioned you were worried about how I might react. I wanted to make sure you knew I was okay with it."

She realized he was standing there in the wind and quickly stepped aside. "Come on in. I don't know what it looked like when you

lived here, but Pat said they remodeled the whole complex not too long ago."

He stepped into the foyer and glanced around. "I had furniture in here, but not much. It was kind of a bachelor pad. But since I was in medical school there was none of the partying that goes along with that."

Vivi smiled. "Medical school doesn't leave a whole lot of time for that. Come on in and sit down. I was just making soup. There's plenty if you want some."

Following her into the kitchen area he glanced at the pot that was on the stove. "So that's what that wonderful smell is. I'd love a bowl, if you're sure there's enough."

"Believe me, there is. Have a seat at the bar. I have wine, if you want some, or water or some cola."

"Water will be fine."

She hesitated. "Will it bother you if I have wine with mine?"

"Not at all."

Vivi took down a wineglass and a tumbler from one of Pat and Guilherme's well-stocked cabinets and set them in front of the bar stools and poured the drinks. Cris was sitting there looking far too "right" in the space and she reminded herself that she'd better not get used

to it. He wasn't interested in permanence and there was no way she wanted him to realize how much she cared for him.

He dragged a hand through his hair to get it off his forehead as she got down two bowls and some spoons and set them in front of their spots. "I have some extra cheese if you want yours topped with it."

"However you're having it will be fine."

Well aware that he was watching her every move she got the cheese she'd grated earlier and put it into a bowl and poured some cream into a little pitcher she found in another cabinet. Then she cut slices from a rustic bread she'd purchased at the store and set the pot on top of a trivet. Ladling some of the soup into the two bowls, she came around to sit on the other stool. Right next to him. Somehow this was different from sitting across the table from someone. Sitting next to him felt much more intimate, somehow, as if they'd done this a thousand other times. And back when they'd been an item they would have sat next to each other in the booth of a local diner they liked to go to.

She took a sip of her wine, letting it swirl on her tongue for a moment before swallowing it. "There's bread. And help yourself to the cheese or *nata*. I like to pour a little more into my bowl."

She added some cream to her own soup and then sprinkled some of the cheese on top. He did the same. Then he took a spoonful.

"Wow, delicious. It's been ages since I've had this."

"Thanks. I'm hoping to grow my own poblanos out on the balcony. I use a lot of them when I cook."

She then took a swallow and had to admit it was good. And it had felt good to cook something for herself rather than going out to eat, like she'd grown accustomed to. Estevan liked to eat out. And as weird as it sounded, he seemed to prefer prepackaged food to eating something that was homemade. He'd said it was because his family had rarely eaten out and it felt like a luxury to be able to go out whenever he wanted. They never actually fought about it, because Vivi had tried to keep the peace, something she tended to do to her own detriment. Her dad used to tell her to speak up if she wanted something. But when she'd spoken up about wanting to stay in Valpo, he hadn't listened and insisted that the move had been necessary. And being her normal easygoing self, she hadn't pushed the issue after that. But she'd cried herself to sleep for months after the move.

"I'm a pretty big fan of poblanos myself. My mom used to dry the red ones and grind them into powder to add to dishes. It's one of the things I remember most about her. Her love of cooking."

How he must miss them. "Your parents were always nice to me."

He smiled. "They were nice people. Their deaths were a huge blow."

"I'm sure. I'm so glad your aunt and uncle lived nearby."

He took another spoonful of soup as if contemplating his answer. "Yes. My aunt grieved losing her sister, but they took me in and made sure I knew that I still had family. That I was not alone."

"You're not. You've got a wonderful family who loves you and a sweetheart of a daughter. She looks just like you, you know."

"Really? I don't see it."

Her brows shot up. "Um…curly hair that goes every which way. Check. Long dark lashes. Check. Deep brown eyes. Check. A dimple in her left cheek. Check."

"I'm a bit offended by that comment about my hair going every which way." Even as he said it, he pushed it off his forehead again only to have it drop right back to where it was before.

"I rest my case."

That made him laugh and the sound filled her apartment like nothing she'd ever heard. He was... In. Her. Apartment. She didn't know why, but that seemed so monumental. They didn't have to stay outside and talk. Or find a park. Or sit in a car in order to be alone.

And they could do anything. Without having to hide it.

"So you rest your case about my hair?"

"Yep. I used to wish I had hair just like yours. But it wouldn't have looked nearly as good on me as it does on you."

He spooned the last of the soup into his mouth and watched her for a minute. "So you think I have crazy hair, but that it looks good."

"Exactly." She laughed, because when he put it like that it did sound kind of ludicrous. "See? It makes perfect sense."

She got back to the reason he'd come by in the first place. "So you really don't mind me renting this place?"

"No. And my aunt says you are the perfect person for the place. She knew it from the moment that she heard you were looking for an apartment. She was going to save it to show you last, but she just couldn't. She was afraid you'd settle for something else and never get to see it."

"I didn't know that. Well, I'm glad she showed it to me first, because it really is perfect for me. Right down to the location and everything." She used her bread to mop up the last bit of soup and ate it, then motioned at the pot. "There's plenty more of everything."

"I think I'm okay for now. It really was good." He put his napkin on the bar next to his bowl. "I don't want to hold you up, though. I'm sure you're ready to put your feet up and be done for the night."

Suddenly she didn't want him to leave, and she wasn't sure why. Maybe because she would likely never have him here again. Never again have him share a meal that she'd made. And it felt like those were things that should have happened a long time ago, but that they never got the chance to experience together.

And despite everything, she grieved that loss more than she grieved the rest of it.

"I could make us some coffee and we could drink it on the veranda, if you have time." She realized she was forgetting something. "You probably have to get home to Gabi, though."

"My aunt and uncle took her to Santiago for the day shopping, so she's spending the night with them."

"Got it." She stood up. "So…coffee?"

"Yes, that sounds good. It's been a while since I've just taken my time eating or had a coffee after dinner. Life is so busy. Too busy."

"I know what you mean." She got up and ground some beans she'd bought just the other day and loaded her French press with those and poured boiling water over them. As she waited for the coffee to brew, she got out mugs, cream and sugar.

Chileans traditionally drank more tea than coffee, but Vivi's mom had always made coffee thanks to her American roots and her dad had followed along and started drinking the beverage as well. So it was kind of surprising that when she met Cris all those years ago, he liked coffee as well, even way back then before the coffee industry started growing.

Pushing the plunger of her coffee maker down to trap the spent ground at the bottom of the carafe, she divided the brew between the two mugs, offering him cream and sugar and finding that he still liked his black rather than sweet like she did. "Are you okay with going outside? I know it's warm, but there's normally a nice breeze blowing up here."

"I know. I used to live here, remember?" He smiled. "And yes, I'm great with that."

They took their mugs and went outside, sitting at the café table that sat just outside the sliding patio door. It was already dark out and there were lights on at the pool and a few people were in it, enjoying the night. But even with that, it was still quiet and there was a peacefulness to the complex that she found surprising. But maybe that was one of its best-selling features.

They sat in the dark and drank their coffee in silence for several minutes, before he said, "I used to love sitting out here after a hard day of school. I would just keep the light off and drink tea. Or coffee. Or whatever I had available and just decompress after the day. I won't tell you the number of times that I fell asleep with my head on this very café table."

"Oh, so this was here when you lived here?"

"It was one of the few things that they kept. It brings back memories."

Her chest ached for what he must have gone through back then. "I hope not all the memories are bad."

"No, not all of them." He glanced at her for a long time. "Definitely not all of them."

She held her breath. Was he talking about twenty years ago? Because when she looked back at all of the upheaval they had both gone through it was hard to find the good among the rubble of the bad.

"Which ones?" She was genuinely curious.

"The ones of us together in the park come to mind. It was where I think I felt the closest to you. Where we could be ourselves completely because there were none of our family or classmates around. I had you all to myself."

That surprised her. But in a good way. "I felt the same. It was kind of 'our' place. Where we went to talk, to laugh, to…"

Her voice died away because she'd been about to say where they'd gone to kiss. It had been. That had been a big part of their time there. And when someone looked at them askance, they simply moved to a different spot in the park and started up all over again.

"Yes. I remember it all. And more."

Her fingers slid across the table and clasped his. "It was good back then, wasn't it? Carefree and simple."

"It was." He suddenly leaned across the table and pressed his lips to hers. And there was no hesitation on her part. She kissed him back with all that she had in her, reveling in the way his fingers slid into the strands of hair at the back of her head, at the way his tongue almost immediately sought entrance.

And she could deny him nothing. And would instead give him anything he wanted. For as long as he wanted.

CHAPTER NINE

CRIS WASN'T SURE exactly what had triggered it. This deep-seated need to kiss her. He didn't know if it was the food or the peace and quiet of the veranda or if it was just the memories of their time together. But something sparked it. He'd halfway expected to kiss her for a second or two and then back off, but Vivi was evidently having none of it. She was immediately kissing him back as if she'd been waiting for this very thing.

Maybe she had been. And maybe he had as well.

And when he stood from the table and held out his hand, she immediately put hers into it. And this time it was Vivi who led the way into the space and moved to the bedroom with a certainty that said he didn't have to ask her if this was what she wanted. Because it obviously was.

And there'd been no planning. No matchmaking. No half-thought-out plans. He hadn't come here with the intent of making love to her. Had simply come here to put her mind at ease. But he wasn't sad that it was morphing into something else. He'd had a hard time putting their last session out of his mind and had ended up not only thinking about it but dreaming about it. Long lazy dreams that had them tracing patterns over each other's bodies.

They got to the room and where there was urgency and rushing the last time, it was obvious that this was going to be about taking it easy and getting it right. Not that they hadn't done that last time, but so much of it seemed like a blur. It had moved with a speed that was hard to savor when looked back on.

If it was going to become a memory, he wanted it to be a long sliding of bodies together. Of kissing deep into the night. And this was the first time that he'd been okay with it happening in someone's home rather than in the impersonal space of a hotel. And it was something he didn't need to examine. Not right now.

Vivi undressed him with slow movements that were intoxicating and sensual. What skin she uncovered, she kissed. His shoulders. His pecs….his nipples. And his body went rigid at the intimate touch.

His shirt fell to the floor and she started on his belt buckle, moving to undo the button and fly on his slacks. And then she was pushing them down his hips until he could kick his legs free of them as well as his shoes.

"My turn."

She smiled a slow sexy smile that made his mouth go dry. "No. It was your turn last time. I want equal billing." Her fingers slid into his briefs and found him with ease.

And then she proceeded to show him in ways he hadn't dared to imagine that she was going to get as much as she could from him before she finally set him free.

Vivi woke up first and felt the pressure of his arm around her waist. She'd fallen asleep just like this with her back pressed against his warm chest, their legs tangled together in the bedclothes. It felt so right that it made her want to weep. If they could have stayed together here in some kind of limbo while the rest of the world stood still, she would have gladly done it.

She retrieved her watch from the side table and looked at it. It was just now eight o'clock.

She wasn't due at the hospital for another two hours, although she wasn't sure what time Cris's day started. Maybe he had today off for some reason.

Trying not to wake him, she slid free of his embrace and got into the shower, soaping her hair and body before leaning her head back and rinsing the shampoo from it. A cool breeze from somewhere made her blink and she realized that the door to the shower stall was open and Cris was standing there in the opening. And what he wanted was very evident in the rigid flesh that stood ready.

The man was evidently insatiable.

She thought they'd done as much as they possibly could last night. But it looked like he was out to prove her wrong.

She held her hand out to him and then froze when the buzzer to her front door went off. Oh, God. It couldn't be. Not now.

She jumped out of the shower and threw him a towel. "Hide in the bedroom."

"Hide? Are you kidding me? Are we back in high school? Just tell whoever it is to get lost and then you come back in here. Or better yet, we can just ignore it."

"My car is down there. They'll know."

This time he looked at her in a way that

made her cringe. "Are you expecting a specific person?"

"No. But if it's who I think it might be, you're not going to want to be caught *in flagrante*."

"*Maldicion*. Are you saying it could be my aunt?"

"I don't know." The buzzer rang again. "Hurry."

This time he grabbed the towel and wrapped it around himself and then stalked into the bedroom. "Do not tell her I'm here."

"I won't. Of course I won't."

She was sick that he would even think that.

She pulled on her long terry robe and cinched the belt tight, wrapping her wet hair in a towel. Then she padded to the door and peered through the peephole. It was indeed Cris's aunt and she wasn't alone. Her sense of nausea grew. He was not going to be happy. In fact, he was probably going to regret ever coming over here. But there was nothing she could do about that now. Pat had to know she was home.

She opened the door and forced a smile. "Hi, you guys. Sorry for not getting to the door earlier. I was showering."

"No, we're the ones who should be sorry.

But Gabi wanted to bring you something we bought in Santiago before she has to go to school."

The child was practically dancing at Pat's side. "Show her!"

"I'm trying to, Gabs. Give me a chance." She pulled a bag out of her purse and gave it to Gabi. "You show her. Then we have to go or you're going to be late."

Gabi opened the bag and brought out a kitchen towel. When she turned it over, Vivi's eyes watered for no good reason. Displayed in bold print were the words My Favorite Nurse Lives Here.

"Oh, Gabi, I love it. Thank you so much." She leaned down to hug the child. "I'll hang it in my kitchen."

"Can I see where?"

Before anyone could stop her, Gabi had walked through the living room and into the kitchen. Pat mouthed, "Sorry."

"It's okay." But inside she was panicking that Gabi might go and open the bedroom door. Taking the little towel, she opened it up and threaded it through the first door handle she could find for one of the cabinet doors. "Right here. This is where I'll keep it. Where I can see it right as I walk into the kitchen."

"You really like it?"

"Yes, Gabi. I love it. Very much. Thank you."

Pat took hold of the girl's hand. "Now it's time for us to go." She drew Gabi to the door and went out, looking into the parking lot and then stopping still. Her head slowly swiveled back toward her. "Oh, Vivi. I'm so sorry. I had no idea. If I had we never would have come."

There was no denying it. The woman had obviously spotted Cris's car parked next to hers. "Please don't let her see it."

"See what?" Gabi asked.

"Nothing important. I'll tell you later." She turned to go, towing the child behind her as they made their way to the stairwell. Then they were gone. And she hoped and prayed the little girl did not see her father's car parked in her lot. Or realized that he'd just spent the night in her bed. Because Gabi's "favorite nurse" might have to let her down hard when she found out that Daddy and Vivi were probably not going to wind up together. Especially not after what had just happened.

But there was nothing to do but go and face the music.

When she got to the bedroom, she found Cris there fully dressed. Even though she already knew they weren't going to take up where they left off, the resigned look on his face made her want to weep.

"Did you know they were coming?"

"I swear I didn't. I mean I know Pat was planning on coming sometime, but there was no specific time or day."

"They know, don't they?"

"Pat saw your car and guessed. I asked her to make sure Gabi didn't see it."

"Mierda!" He came into the kitchen and spotted the towel, his eyes closing. "I asked you not to let her get attached."

The words were so soft and so even that they made her swallow hard. And when he came back into the dining room he touched something on the table, picking it up and turning it over before his head came up and he fixed her with a look before setting it back down. She moved closer and realized it was her ring. The one he'd given her when they were seventeen.

God, he must think she'd planned all of this. The ring. The night spent in her bed. His aunt catching them this morning.

"I didn't! Do you think I would purposely set out to ingratiate myself with an innocent child? I've only seen her a handful of times and you were there for two of those times. First at the hospital and then at the picnic."

"You're right. I know you wouldn't." He shook his head. "I can't do this. I'm truly sorry, Vivi, but I can't. Gabi is everything to me and I won't see her hurt. I won't let her experience any more loss than what she's already experienced."

A thread of anger came over her. "You say that like you think I'm going to try to trap you in something you have no desire to be a part of. I think I already assured you that I wasn't going to do that. The ring fell out of a box of mementos, that's it. But because you're worried about it, I think it's better if we make sure we're not alone again. If you don't want it, then don't put yourself in situations where things might just flame out of control."

She went on. "We'll see each other at work and that's it. You can tell your aunt whatever you want to. She knows you're here, and she's not stupid. She knows exactly what we were up to. If you want to tell her I changed my mind, feel free. If you want to tell her it meant nothing, that's fine too. Because really it's the truth. We had sex. So what? You once gave me that little ring, if you remember, and it also turned out to mean nothing in the end."

"Vivi—"

"No. Just go." She sighed, suddenly more tired than she'd been in ages. "I can't do this again. I can't think that things are going to work out only to discover that there was nothing there. I came to Valpo to get away from a relationship that had gone wrong. I'm not about to step into another one that I already *know* is wrong."

When he acted like he might say something else she just shook her head. "Please, Cris. Just go."

And so he did. And rather than watch as yet another man walked out on her without a backward glance, she shut the door so she wouldn't have to look.

Cris had done two more surgeries with Vivi over the week that followed. But he hadn't seen her in the last two days. Not a word passed between them that didn't have to do with the procedures at hand. Pat had handed over Gabi without a word the day of her encounter with Vivi. She never said anything about seeing his car or that she knew he'd been there. She simply gave him a hug and then kissed Gabi goodbye. But as she'd left she said, "Don't hurt your daughter just because you're afraid." And then she was gone.

He'd pondered her words for the next week, even though he already knew exactly what she was talking about. But Pat wasn't the one who had to live with the fear of losing someone else. With the fear of his daughter being devastated when someone she cared about left, either by dying or by just moving out of their sphere.

So no, he wasn't going to risk it. Not again.

But he did owe Vivi the courtesy of telling her why he couldn't take things any further. But when he went to the nurses' station, he was told that she'd left early and had said she was headed to Santiago for a while.

She was going back there?

Evidently. And it was because if him. It had to be. And if he hadn't already felt bad enough about the way things had ended, he now felt even worse. He'd had no business letting things go as far as they had. But he hadn't been able to resist her or the lure of the might-have-been.

Well, now he knew what could have been and he wished he'd never ventured into those waters. Because his feet did not want to pull free of those last few inches of liquid. Did not want that last droplet to dry into nothingness.

But why? Why did it matter so very much?

The truth hit him so hard that he had to sit down. Had to cradle his head in his hands to deal with the throbbing pain that pierced through his skull.

He loved her. Hell, he'd probably fallen back in love with her that first day he looked across the operating table and realized that Vivi was back in Valpo.

But what did he do with all of the other "stuff"? He'd lost both his parents and his wife to tragedies that had been none of their doing. What if it happened again? What if he couldn't stop that fear from bubbling up every time he looked at her? Every time he took her in his arms and wondered if this was the last time?

Well, it was either somehow find a way of dealing with it and trust that Gabi would be okay no matter what happened. Or he needed to shut Vivi out of his life once and for all.

Hell, he did not know what to do. Or which way to turn.

But weren't there more ways to experience loss? And if you did the wrong thing, could you actually *cause* the loss that you hoped to avoid?

He blinked as that realization washed over him like a flood. If he pushed Vivi away, he was effectively doing the very thing that would cause Gabi pain. She loved Vivi already. It was as if she was able to read who Vivi was and knew that she was the "right" person to complete their family. And if he didn't see that and recognize it for what it was, he would be the reason she experienced a loss that would undoubtedly affect her. And what would be gained in doing that?

Nothing. Absolutely nothing.

He couldn't see anything right now, but his own stupidity. But what if he wasn't seeing past his own lust? Past his own desire to be part of a relationship again? He was too close to the situation. But he knew someone who wasn't. And so he drew out his phone and dialed the number of the people who had helped him weather some pretty awful crises. Maybe they could help prevent him from creating another one. This one of his own making.

"Uncle Guilherme? Do you and Aunt Pat have time for me to come over while Gabi is in school? I need to talk to you about something. And if you say what I think you're going to say, I want to talk to my daughter and ask what she thinks about it all."

"Of course, Cris. Come over now. We're home. We'll always be home."

Vivi lounged by the pool of her parents' rental house and tried to make sense out of what had happened. She'd moved to Valpo to get away from Estevan only to run smack dab into another situation that was just as bad, if not worse.

Because Cris was the real deal, where Estevan had only been a shadow that had looked real until you peered under the surface and saw that it was all just pretend. Playacting. Their relationship had never been made of the stuff that lasted. If she and Cris had made a go of it, she knew it would have worked.

But they would never get the chance, because Cris wasn't willing to risk failure or whatever the hell else he was afraid of. Yes, he'd suffered some terrible losses. But so did thousands of other people in this country. And most of them didn't give up on…life. And that's what he'd done. Just as surely as Roni had after he'd had his knee replacement and realized he'd never play soccer again. But Roni had regained his footing and was finding a way to deal with his loss rather than just saying no to everything good that came his way.

And she and Cris would be good together. She knew they would be. If only he had been willing to take a risk.

She flipped over onto her back, trying to force herself not to think about him anymore. Because in the end it did nothing but make the ache in her chest come back.

Putting her arm over her eyes, she tried to focus on the warmth of the sun as it played across her skin.

When she'd shown up on her mom and dad's doorstep, they hadn't asked what was wrong; they just pulled her into their arms and let her cry it out. In the end, it was her dad who'd asked her if she was sure she wanted to give up on Cris. She simply replied she didn't know. But she hoped she'd come to a decision by the time she left Santiago.

She lay there for what seemed like ages, knowing she should probably go in and help her mom prepare lunch, but the sun felt so good. So healing. And right now, it was what she needed.

A chill came over her, and she blinked to see if clouds were gathering. Then her breathing stopped when she realized it wasn't clouds that were blocking the sun. It was the very man she'd come here to forget. Or at least figure out what to do about.

"Cris? Is Gabi okay?"

He sat on the lower part of the lounge chair and faced her. "Not really."

She sat up in a rush and found herself inches from his mouth. "What's wrong with her?"

He touched her hair, his warm fingers sifting through it. "The same thing that's wrong with me. We miss you, Vivi."

"But you..." Confusion rolled over her like a wave, and she couldn't figure out what he was even trying to say. "You said you didn't want me near her. That you couldn't do this."

He closed his eyes for a brief moment before reopening them. "I know I did. And I was wrong. I see that now. I even went and talked with my aunt and uncle and they assured me that coming here was not the wrong thing to do. It was the only right thing I *could* do under the circumstances.

"Circumstances?"

"I love you, Vivi. I know that now. And I'm hoping I'm not too late...that maybe you feel the same way about me. That maybe you can forgive me for pushing away something good. Something healing. Because I realize now that I *have* been healing. And it took you leaving to make me realize it."

She tilted her head, not moving out of his proximity. "I didn't leave. Not really. I just came here to do some thinking."

"And if that thinking had you wondering if maybe you should leave for good? I don't think I could endure that a second time. I lost you once, Vivi. I don't want to lose you again. Please say you'll come back to Valpo."

Her fingers went up to touch his cheeks, still not positive that he was really here, but hoping beyond hope that this wasn't a dream. The warmth of his skin, though, told her that she was very much awake and that Cris was no phantom. He was here. Telling her that he loved her and that he wanted her to come back to Valparaiso.

"Why? Why do you want me to come back?"

"Because I want my aunt to lose the tenant that she just signed. I want you to move out and move in with me and Gabi. I want to spend my life with you. The place doesn't matter. What does matter is that you and me and Gabi are together."

"Does she know you're here?"

"Yes. I told her in words she could understand, and she's even more excited about you coming to live with us than she is about Mollete."

"Moll…who?"

"Never mind. Just know that she's all in favor of it."

She licked her lips, afraid this was all going to fall apart somehow. "Are you sure? You're not going to change your mind in a month's time?"

"I'm not going to change my mind. That much I can tell you. I don't know exactly what it'll look like…this life that we'll share. But what I do know is that I don't want to do life without you. As long as you say yes."

She smiled and kissed his mouth. It was a long time before either one of them came up for air, but when they did, he pulled her to him in a hug that threatened to crush all her bones. And she loved it.

"I don't have a ring yet, but when I do…"

"That's where you're wrong." She didn't give him a chance to say anything—she just walked into the house, very aware of his eyes on her bikini-clad form. She went to her room and picked up the thing he'd seen on her dining room table. The thing she'd brought back to Santiago to help her make a decision about her future.

She sat down next to him and opened her palm, revealing the thin gold band with its tiny crystals. "I couldn't leave it behind on the table. It just seemed...wrong."

He took it from her and examined it. "I can't believe you kept this all these years."

She nodded. "Not because I ever thought this would happen, but because I couldn't let go of that little piece of my childhood. I wanted to remember. Because as hard as it was, those memories were good. Some of the best times of my life happened in Valpo."

"Are you sure, Vivi?"

"Very sure."

He slid the ring on her finger and looked at it for a long moment before lifting her hand and kissing it. "It still fits."

"I know."

"In that case, will you marry me?"

"I will. And I don't need any band other than this one. It's the only one I want."

He wrapped his arm around her shoulders and pulled her against his chest, resting his chin on her head. "Your dad isn't going to make you move again, is he?"

She laughed. "No. And if he even tried, I'd tell him to forget it. He actually apologized yesterday for any part he may have played in our rift. I assured him that if things were meant to be they'd work out. And it looks like maybe they are." She twisted her head to kiss his shoulder. "He's happy for us, this time."

"He did seem a little more pleased to see me than he was the last time we saw each other." He leaned over and pressed his cheek to hers. "I want to spend my life with you. Um…is it too soon to talk babies?"

That made her laugh. "Yes, it is. But I'm not saying it's off the table. But let's give us a chance to get to know each other again. This time knowing it's for keeps."

"For keeps. I like that."

"For keeps," she agreed. "Shall we seal the deal?"

"Out here on the deck? I don't think your dad would approve."

She took his hand and helped him to his feet. "No. Not on the deck." She nodded at the water. "That was more what I had in mind."

Still holding his hand, she walked to the edge and jumped into the pool, her grip on his hand hauling him into the water with her. When they bobbed to the surface she turned and kissed his mouth, treading water. "I love you, Cris. And I always will."

"I'm going to hold you to that. For the rest of our lives."

EPILOGUE

THE PORTILLO SKI resort was as beautiful as she'd imagined it would be, and she couldn't have asked for a better place to honeymoon. Vivi had even ventured onto one of the ski lifts yesterday, although she'd gripped Cris's hand so hard that she'd probably bruised it.

And the snow… *Dios,* the snow. It was white and soft and it sparkled under the stars tonight. Just like the little crystals in her ring. It was a magical place, and she never wanted to leave.

But they would have to soon. Gabi was staying part-time with Cris's aunt and uncle and part of the time with her folks, who were camped out in the apartment she and Cris had just bought. They'd wanted a new start for their new life. They'd waited six months to get married, just to give Gabi and themselves time to adjust to being a family. But there'd never been any doubt that it would work this time. Because they were willing to put in the hard work. They were worth it. Their love was worth it.

And there were talks of adding a baby to the mix, both agreeing to start trying as soon as they got home.

Roni had made it through physical therapy and the new program at the hospital was up and running and was going even better than she could have imagined. And none of her fears had materialized. It was a team effort and Roni had welcomed any and all advice, and instead of coaching a big professional team, he had opted to coach school kids who were just learning about the game. He said it fulfilled him in a way that his career never had.

She was glad for him. And glad for the kids whose lives would be enriched by the time and effort he put into them.

And Clara's dad had unexpectedly come out of his coma a month after the accident and surpassed all of the predictions, seeming to have made a full recovery. Her big strong husband had actually shed a few tears as he told her the news. And she loved him all the more for that display of emotion.

Although their separation twenty years ago

had been difficult, she had to believe that things had worked out the way they should have. She insisted on having a large picture of Lidia displayed on a wall in their living room and she intended to scatter photos of her with a baby Gabi throughout the house.

It was twenty years after the fact, but Vivi knew they were meant to be together. It was the timing that had been the question. They had both grown into the people they needed to be to make a strong healthy marriage and it made them appreciate being together even more.

She gathered some snow in her hand and pressed it into a ball. "Do you think we can take one of these back with us?"

"Hmm…probably. But it might not be in the same form by the time we get home."

"True. Maybe I'll just leave it here, where it belongs."

He wrapped his arms around her and cupped his hands around the snow. "I'm glad you're where you belong."

"Me too. I wouldn't want to do life without you."

He kissed the top of her head. "You don't have to. I love you, *querida*."

She twisted until she was facing him, the snowball falling to the ground. "How much?"

"Too much. Too damned much."

"Really? Maybe you can show me exactly how much 'too damned much' is." She sent him a smile and hoped he caught the inference.

He did, judging from the way he grabbed her hand and started towing her to the nearest entrance. "Oh, it's a lot. A whole damned lot."

Vivi laughed, the sound carrying across the grounds of the resort and into the night. "That's exactly what I'm counting on."

* * * * *

*If you enjoyed this story,
check out these other great reads from
Tina Beckett*

New York Nights with Mr. Right
Las Vegas Night with Her Best Friend
Reunion with the ER Doctor
ER Doc's Miracle Triplets

All available now!

Get up to 4 Free Books!

We'll send you 2 free books from each series you try PLUS a free Mystery Gift.

FREE Value Over $25

Both the **Harlequin Presents** and **Harlequin Medical Romance** series feature exciting stories of passion and drama.

YES! Please send me 2 FREE novels from Harlequin Presents or Harlequin Medical Romance and my FREE gift (gift is worth about $10 retail). After receiving them, if I don't wish to receive any more books, I can return the shipping statement marked "cancel." If I don't cancel, I will receive 6 brand-new larger-print novels every month and be billed just $7.19 each in the U.S., or $7.99 each in Canada, or 4 brand-new Harlequin Medical Romance Larger-Print books every month and be billed just $7.19 each in the U.S. or $7.99 each in Canada, a savings of 20% off the cover price. It's quite a bargain! Shipping and handling is just 50¢ per book in the U.S. and $1.25 per book in Canada.* I understand that accepting the 2 free books and gift places me under no obligation to buy anything. I can always return a shipment and cancel at any time. The free books and gift are mine to keep no matter what I decide.

Choose one: ☐ **Harlequin Presents Larger-Print** (176/376 BPA G36Y)   ☐ **Harlequin Medical Romance** (171/371 BPA G36Y)   ☐ **Or Try Both!** (176/376 & 171/371 BPA G36Z)

Name (please print)

Address   Apt. #

City   State/Province   Zip/Postal Code

Email: Please check this box ☐ if you would like to receive newsletters and promotional emails from Harlequin Enterprises ULC and its affiliates. You can unsubscribe anytime.

Mail to the Harlequin Reader Service:
IN U.S.A.: P.O. Box 1341, Buffalo, NY 14240-8531
IN CANADA: P.O. Box 603, Fort Erie, Ontario L2A 5X3

Want to explore our other series or interested in ebooks? Visit www.ReaderService.com or call 1-800-873-8635.

HPHM25